Charles-Albert Moré

The chevalier de Pontgibaud

A French volunteer of the war of independence

Charles-Albert Moré

The chevalier de Pontgibaud
A French volunteer of the war of independence

ISBN/EAN: 9783744646802

Printed in Europe, USA, Canada, Australia, Japan

Cover: Foto ©ninafisch / pixelio.de

More available books at **www.hansebooks.com**

THE CHEVALIER DE PONTGIBAUD

A FRENCH VOLUNTEER

OF THE

WAR OF INDEPENDENCE

TRANSLATED AND EDITED BY

ROBERT B. DOUGLAS

Author of
"*Sophie Arnould: Actress and Wit*", *The Life and Times of Madame du Barry*", *etc., etc.*

WITH AN ENGRAVED PORTRAIT BY THEVENIN

PARIS
CHARLES CARRINGTON
13 FAUBOURG MONTMARTRE
1898

"The Story of my life,
From year to year, the battles, sieges, fortunes,
That I have passed."

OTHELLO, Act. i. sc. 3.

(SECOND EDITION.)

PREFACE.

The Chevalier de Pontgibaud was one of the gallant little band of Frenchmen, who, "sick for breathing and exploit", crossed the Atlantic to aid the American colonists to gain their independence. Like most of his companions, he was a mere lad, courageous, adventurous, high-spirited, light-hearted, and cool-headed, but he united to these ordinary attributes of the French gentleman, one which his comrades did not possess, or had no opportunity of developing. He seems to have been a shrewd observer of men and events, and he had a keen sense of humour.

It was not probable that a youth barely out of his teens and thinking more of his own liberty than the cause in which he was engaged, should have noted his impressions at the time. They were written down more than forty years later, but that will not detract from the value of a book which gives vivid pen-portraits of men about whom much has been written but of whom much yet remains to be written.

Concerning the author's life, little need be added to what he tells us, but I am indebted to his great-great-nephew, the Comte de Pontgibaud, for some details which are not to be found in the book. The Chevalier de

Pontgibaud married—31 July 1789—a daughter of Maréchal de Vaux, and the widow of Comte de Fougières, *maréchal de camp*. He was deeply attached to her, and only survived her a few months. She died in 1836 and he in 1837. From the time of his return to France (1814) till his wife's death, he resided at 6, Place Royale, Paris, but afterwards removed to the residence of his nephew, Comte de Pontgibaud, 32, Rue des Tournelles, where he died.

He was a genial, kind-hearted man, and it is related of him that in his later days he never left home without a pocketful of five-francs pieces, one of which coins he would bestow on each poor person he met. "As I want for nothing myself," he said, "let me do all I can for poor people who do want." Indeed had it not been for his charitable disposition he would never in all likelihood have written his book. His cousin, Mme de Lavau, who was interested in many charitable works, said to him one day, "My dear cousin, you have had such an adventurous career that an account of the principal events of your life would make a most interesting book. I would give away the copies as prizes in a lottery, and I warrant we should get a large sum for one of my charities." The proposal was perhaps hardly flattering to the author, but he was too kind-hearted to refuse, and the book was duly written. He even permitted a relative to pad out the volume by the addition of some singularly dull letters, which, being devoid of all interest, have been omitted from the present translation.

The Mémoires du Comte de M——— (the writer was then known as the Comte de Moré) has become a rare book, and appears to have been unknown to many of the historians and biographers whose writings relate to the War of Independence and the actors concerned in it.

That the book is rare and rather valuable is due to the "book-maniacs", who have snapped-up every available copy, not on account of any interest in the book or its author, but because of—the printer! A certain young man had persuaded his relatives to set him up in business as a printer, but in a little over a year he contrived to lose more than 150,000 francs. He threw up the business in disgust, and resolved to make his living by the pen. To prove that he was better fitted to compose with the pen than with the "stick", it needs but to cite his name,— Honoré de Balzac! Even a book which had the honour of proceeding from the novelist's unprofitable press has acquired a fictitious value.

Both as the Chevalier de Pontgibaud and the Marquis de Moré, the author had the good sense to keep out of politics, and his name occurs but rarely in memoirs and histories of the day. In Vatel's *Vie de Madame du Barry* he is mentioned as being present at a dinner party to which she was invited. The incident is related in the MS. Memoirs of Comte Dufort de Cheverny. "Seeing that the Chevalier wore the Order of Cincinnatus, she told us the following story. 'When I was at Versailles, I had the six tallest and best looking footmen that could be found, but the noisiest, laziest rascals that ever lived. The ring-leader of them gave me so much trouble that I was obliged to send him away. The war in America was then beginning, and he asked for letters of recommendation. I gave them, and he left me with a well filled purse, and I was glad to get rid of him. A year ago he came to see me, and he was wearing the Order of Cincinnatus.' We all laughed at the story, except the Chevalier de Pontgibaud."

On the fly leaf of a book in the Library at Clermont

Ferrand there are also some MS. notes—supposed to be written by Comte Thomas d'Espinchal—relating to the Chevalier de Pontgibaud. It is there stated that the Chevalier furnished Talleyrand with the means of returning to France by lending him 600 louis. It is not improbable, and as the Ex-Bishop would be absolutely certain to forget the obligation, this may account for certain severe remarks about Talleyrand to be found towards the close of the present volume.

In editing the Chevalier's Memoirs I have done little more than identify the personages named only by initials, and supply notes concerning them, correct one or two dates, and strike out a passage or two that was not according to modern taste. As a translator I have endeavoured, as I always do, to render the original as faithfully as could be, and preserve the style and spirit of the author. The only liberty I have taken with the text is to cut up some of the sentences, for a few of them were of an inordinate length. If it should be found that the style is not always of the purest, it should be remembered that the Chevalier was a man of action, and was fighting for the freedom of America at an age when less adventurous youths are quietly pursuing their studies.

ROBT. B. DOUGLAS.

PARIS, 10th January 1897.

CONTENTS.

Chapter I.

Birth—Early days—Education—Out in the world—Sent to the prison of Pierre-en-Cize by order of the King. 1

Chapter II.

Eighteen months in prison—A plan of escape successfully carried out—Armed resistance—Sheltered by a Lyons merchant—Arrival in Auvergne—A family compact—A compromise effected—Departure to join the so-called "insurgent army" in America. 13

Chapter III.

Wrecked in Chesapeake Bay—Williamsburg—Mr. Jefferson—Aspect of the country between Williamsburg and the camp at Valley Forges—Description of the American Army—Welcomed by Marquis de la Fayette—He appoints me his aide-de-camp—My mission to the Oneida Indians—American ideas of the French—The camp at Valley Forges—General Howe's dog—Attempted sortie of the British Army from Philadelphia—The passage of the Schuylkill, and return—Our ambulance surgeon—Evacuation of Philadelphia—Defeat at Rareton Rivers—Battle and Victory at Monmouth—New York blockaded—Arnold's treason—Arrest, trial, and execution of Major André—The Earl of Carlisle and Marquis de la Fayette—Comte d'Estaing before New York—Siege of Newport, Rhode Island, by Gen. Sullivan—I am charged with the re-victualling of the French fleet—The siege of Newport raised—Our departure for France on board the frigate "Alliance"—A storm and its consequences—Mutiny on board—Capture of a British cruiser—Arrival at Brest. 33

CHAPTER IV.

I visit my father, and am restored to his good graces—Arrival in Paris—Welcomed by all my relatives—Unexpected appointment as deputy-captain—Ordered to Lorient—Paul Jones and Captain Landais—Counter orders—Re-embark on frigate "Alliance" to rejoin Washington's army—In the absence of Paul Jones, the command of the frigate is given to Landais—He becomes insane during the voyage—Removed from his command by order of the passengers—The campaign of 1781—Siege of York Town—The Capitulation of Cornwallis—End of the American war on the Continent—I return to France on the "Ariel", commanded by Chevalier de Capellis—We fight and capture the British vessel "Dublin"—We enter Corunna in triumph—Fêtes, Balls, etc.—A religious difficulty—We narrowly escape figuring in an auto-da-fé—The "Ariel" weighs anchor—Arrival at Lorient. 77

CHAPTER V.

Proposed expedition to Senegal—A visit to Pierre-en-Cize—The reception I met with there—The celebrity I had left behind me—Institution of the order of Cincinnatus, which I am one of the first to receive—The pleasures of peace, mathematics and the violin—Expedition to Cochin-China—An Oriental Young Pretender—Eastern presents—The year 1789—Physical and political signs of an approaching Revolution—Infatuation of the people at Versailles and Paris—Delille—Nostradamus—Cazotte—La Fayette and my French comrades of the order of Cincinnatus side with the Revolutionary party—I emigrate with my brother—The campaign in Champagne—The retreat—We arrive in Switzerland and establish ourselves at Lausanne—An account of the members of our little family—How an important house of business was founded—Unexpected news—I am called to the United States to receive ten thousand dollars, back pay and interest—I embark at Hamburg and go to receive my money. 96

CHAPTER VI.

My third voyage to the United States—Philadelphia transformed into a new Sidon—The same simplicity of manners—Mr. MacHenry, Secretary of War—M. Duportail—Moreau de Saint-Méry—I meet my old friends again—A triple partnership with Senator Morris at the head of it—Burke's prophecy—Plans proposed to me—Viscount Noailles—The Bishop of Autun—

A mission to the Directory to claim an indemnity—Marino, the pastry-cook, and M. de Volney—The Princes of Orleans—An elephant with a French driver—A trip to New York—Colonel Hamilton—Past, present, and future of the United States—I meet the Chevalier de la C——Our recollections of M. de la Fayette—His escape from the fortress of Olmutz—Dr. Bollman—My return to Europe and arrival at Hamburg. 122

Chapter VII.

Arrival at Hamburg—Departure for France—I become a smuggler at Antwerp—Condition of France—My residence in France—Departure for Trieste—Joseph la Brosse, the banker—The Governors Junot, Bertrand, Fouché (Duke of Otranto)—Gustavson, King of Sweden—Jérôme Bonaparte 156

BIOGRAPHICAL NOTES 193

A FRENCH VOLUNTEER

OF THE

WAR OF INDEPENDENCE.

CHAPTER I.

Birth—Early days—Education—Out in the world—Sent to the prison of Pierre-en-Cize by order of the King.

My father—César de Moré Chaliers, Comte de Pontgibaud—has often informed me that I came into the world on 21st April 1758.* My mother, whose maiden name was Marie Charlotte de Salaberry, was, I believe, at that time a young and pretty woman, but I can recollect very little about her, as she died whilst I was still very young, from a shock caused by being suddenly told some bad news.

I derive my family title from the noble old castle in which my father and mother lived.

The château possessed battlements, solid walls, towers

---

* See note A, p. 193, as to the actual words employed in the original.

black with age, and of undoubted historic interest, but it was not a cheerful residence all the same.

My father was lord of the small town of Pontgibaud, and a good number of parishes round, and united in his own person all the feudal rights of lay and clerical patronage,—for he nominated the *curés* of most of the neighbouring villages. The Comte and Comtesse de Chaliers lived amongst their vassals, who were all dependent on their bounty. No one in the district knew anything about the rights of man, but all did know, and practise, the duties of gratitude and respect. It is a fact that whenever my mother went out, the women and children fell on their knees, and called for heaven's blessing on their lady, and the men, even the oldest, took off their caps when they saw their master and mistress coming, and set the church bells ringing. What harm was there in this interchange of protection on one side, and love on the other? Were they not like children honouring their father and mother?

The huge, old castle overlooked the town, and the fertile valley watered by the Sioule, which stretches far away to the peaks of the Monts d'Or, but like all the valleys in Auvergne, though the view looked so pleasant and peaceful when the elements were at rest, it would sometimes assume in one night a quite different aspect; like the *gaves* of the Pyrenees, our brooks swell into torrents after a single storm, and the floods render the country not only dreary but dangerous.

Custom makes as many victims as imprudence, and the natives of the country really run more risk than travellers, because they are less cautious and more daring. One of our neighbours, a friend of my parents, Comte de Mont——, returning home one night on horseback, missed the ford, which he thought he knew well, and was drowned in the Sioule, which was then in flood. The news of this accident was announced to my mother in too sudden a manner, and gave her a shock from which she never recovered.

With the exception of some trifling incidents, which might have happened to anybody, I can remember nothing that occurred, that deserves to be recounted, from the time that I was weaned till I was ten years old. I had, however, somewhat of the same character which Plutarch remarked in Alcibiades.

I was brought up almost entirely by my maternal grandmother, *la Présidente* de Salaberry. One day at dinner, she said to me,

"My boy, will you have some spinach?"

"I don't like spinach," I replied.

"At your age you ought to like everything, my boy. You will have some spinach."

"I will not eat it."

"You *will* eat it;" and down came my plate with the spinach on it.

My own recollection of the event is hazy, but it appears that I took the plate, and threw the spinach into my grandmother's face,—much to her grief and astonishment, and that of everybody else who was present. She said, "Go to your own room," and I went.

My grandmother,—a very quiet, pious, and respectable old lady,—was far more troubled by the occurrence than I was, for I could only see that it was wrong to try and make me eat spinach when I had said that I didn't like it. The dear old lady put it all down to God's will and the irresponsibility of childhood, and said to her old servant,

"Lepage, go to my grandchild, and tell him to come and beg my pardon; and here is a louis that you may give him from me."

The old servant had no doubt whatever as to the success of his mission, since he had a free pardon and a louis to offer the rebel. He delivered his message, and wound up by saying:

"Come, *monsieur le chevalier!* Here is a louis that your good grandmamma charged me to give you; so come and beg her pardon, and eat your spinach like a good boy."

The louis met with the same fate as the plate, for I threw it in the old man's face.

"Does my grandmother think," I cried, "that I can be bribed into making an apology?"

I suppose I was very proud of this reply, for I often used to think of it afterwards, and do still sometimes, though now I estimate it at what it is worth. As for the little domestic drama, it probably finished like all others of the same kind; the little chevalier made an apology, ate his spinach, and was pardoned by his grandmother,—but I have disliked spinach from that day to this.

But this picture of my youth is only a page from universal history;—an event which might, or does, occur to everybody of the same age and condition.

In 1773 I laid aside the *toga practexta*, and put on the *toga virile*,—or, in other words, I attained my sixteenth year.

Here the storms of life began to beat upon me, for, almost from the beginning, my life has been adventurous. The narration of all that I have suffered, seen, done, and noticed, from Pierre-en-Cize to New York, from Boston to Coblentz, by sea or by land, in both hemispheres, will not be without interest and profit to my friend the reader, whoever he may be, or whatever his age. Fortune set me adrift in a rudderless boat, but I managed to steer it somehow, and am now safe in port, and not dissatisfied on the whole with my long voyage. My bad luck did not astonish me greatly, or my good luck either for that matter; from whence I conclude, that whoever reads me will be more surprised than I either was, or am. My trials began when I was sixteen years old, and I defy M. Azais to classify them in his system of compensations.*

---

* Pierre Hyacinthe Azais, b. 1766, d. 1845. The author of a stupid, and now forgotten book, entitled *The Compensations of Destiny*, which effectually destroyed what little celebrity the author had ever enjoyed.

I must here state that my father had two brothers-in-law, who were excellent uncles to me, and, with the best intentions in the world, did me all the harm they could, but as their intentions were good, I suppose they will not have to answer to God for their misdeeds. The one was the President de Salaberry, and the other Baron d'A——, who, having become a widower, took for his second wife Madame P——, a widow with a grown-up daughter. Madame P——, now my aunt, married her daughter to my elder brother, and I suppose I interfered with her projects and calculations, but at any rate she certainly was not kindly disposed towards me, and by dint of curtain lectures at last persuaded her easy-going, credulous husband, my uncle, to share in her dislike of me. My brother, and my young sister-in-law, had something to do with the schemes of my aunt (her mother, and his mother-in-law), for I have some idea,—in fact I am almost certain,— that her cordial dislike to me was the effect of her maternal tenderness. I was only a "cadet of Auvergne," and my brother was the elder, and by the simple application of one of the four rules of arithmetic,—subtraction,—it appeared evident to her, that if I were out of the way, her daughter would be,—in the event of anything happening to my brother,—sole heiress to the estate, undiminished by the payment of my portion. The prospect seemed tempting: I will not say that it was fair and honourable conduct, but it was not her fault that the end did not crown the work, as will be seen.

After the death of my mother, my father did not revisit Paris, but lived in his old castle, and hoarded up the revenues of his vast domains. I passed, I believe, two or three years at Juilly, under the more or less affectionate care of my uncle, the second husband of a second wife. I picked up some learning,—very much against my will,—under the reverend fathers of the Oratory, but, when I left them, I was not precisely what would be termed a good scholar. If I had shown an inclination to learn anything, it was certainly not Greek or Latin, nor had I much cultivated the flowers of rhetoric.

I then went to college, but resided in my uncle's house, and he was supposed to watch over me. As a matter of fact no one troubled his head about me. To the outside world I appeared to be in the bosom of my own family, and under the watchful eyes of affectionate relatives, but in reality I was left to my own devices, and at sixteen was under no control whatever.

At this critical period of my existence, no one had said what they wanted me to be, nor had I been consulted on the subject. For my own part I neither knew, nor cared. I was sixteen years old, was in Paris, and my own master. I was youthful, vigorous, warm-hearted, inquisitive, and inexperienced, and was fated, like everyone else, to acquire experience at my own expense. With no friends, and no one to guide me, it would have been a miracle

indeed if idleness and want of occupation had not
led me into mischief. But the watchful eyes of
persons who bore me no good-will followed my
every movement. They did not have to wait long
to detect me in some act of thoughtlessness, quickly
followed by other and graver ones, and my aunt
made it her constant care to spitefully exaggerate
all my faults and depict them as crimes to my
uncle, and through him to my father, who was a
hundred leagues away from the capital.

It was made to appear that all the laws of nature
and the divine order of things had been upset,
because a blundering, stupid school-boy of sixteen
had committed a few trifling excesses. Of course,
I had had recourse to the money-lenders. They are
ready enough to come to the aid of any extravagant young man, but I had saved them that trouble
by going to them. The whole extent of my vice
was, that I was acquainted with some young women
of easy morals, and had made some debts, which,
as I was allowed no pocket-money, and was not a
coiner, was hardly a matter for surprise. What
they said, or what they did, or what charges my
aunt brought against me, I know not, but it is
certain that my father was led to regard me as a
monster of iniquity, and not only to give his consent,
but even to order, that a family council should be
called to deliberate on my case. I might have
confessed that I had done neither more nor less
than a young blockhead of sixteen, left to himself

in Paris, might be expected to do, and they must have acknowledged that I was innocent of something like seven-eighths of the capital sins, but my aunt had so mixed up the true with the false, and the false with the probable, that my poor old father did not doubt for an instant but that I was capable of every crime, winding up—since I had not commenced with it—by parricide. I am not overstating the case, absurd as it may sound.

Unhappily for me, all the fathers in Auvergne were just then in a state of fright,—an epidemic of terror had seized them all. There are weak minded people in castles as well as in huts, and fools are to be found in aristocratic drawing-rooms as well as in the sixth floor garrets of city houses. About this time, it was said that many young children had disappeared, and this, coupled with the report that the Dauphin was suffering from some strange malady, led many of the good citizens of Paris to believe that the Prince had been ordered blood baths, and that all the young innocents who were lost had gone to fill his tub,—which caused a good many wooden-headed, wooden-shoed mothers to hide their offspring, as they did in the time of Herod.*

* The writer has made a mistake here. It was Louis XV, not the Dauphin, who was supposed to bathe in the blood of children. The rumour was current in 1750, or twenty-four years earlier than the date here given, and led to riots which were suppressed with some loss of life, and the ringleaders were hanged "on gibbets 40 feet high." See Dareste's *History of France*, Vol vi, p. 416.

At this time also, a rumour was current in Auvergne that young Comte de M—— had tried to poison his father in a dish of eggs and tripe. Whether there was any foundation for this terrible charge, I cannot say, but it is a fact that all the fathers in Auvergne took the matter seriously. Terror reigned under the domestic roof, and there was not a son who was not suspected of parricidal intentions, and all the heads of families talked of living without eating at all, for fear of this fatal dish of eggs and tripe.

Though only sixteen years old, I also came under this terrible imputation, and when, at the request or order of my father, the family council met, it was with no friendly feeling towards me. Without being heard in my own defence,— for the verdict was intended to be an agreeable surprise to me, I suppose,—I was accused, tried, and condemned by all my relatives, with one exception,— that of my cousin german, the Marquis de M——, an officer in the First Regiment of Cavalry. And it cannot be said either that this family meeting was like that of *la fausse Agnes*.* There was my uncle, the *maître des comptes*, my uncle the President de Salaberry, the Marquis de R——, brigadier-general in the King's army, and my wise and respectable cousin M. Th——, captain in the guards. I do not remember what other notabilities were present, except my *belle tante*, wheezing up and down the corridor, and my

---

* An allusion to a once well-known comedy by Destouches, acted at the Comédie Française in 1759.

father, emptying the vials of his paternal wrath, and presiding over the proceedings. My cousin the Marquis de M———, a young soldier accustomed to courts-martial, and knowing how to proportion the punishment to the offence, was the only one who refused to lightly consign to imprisonment,—perhaps for life,—a lad of sixteen. I will, however, do my other relatives the justice to acknowledge that they were sorry afterwards: this they have all since proved to me,—all save my aunt, who has never spoken to me, and whom I have never asked. May God judge her.

It is nevertheless true that, thanks to my kind relations, not one of whom would willingly have done a wrong or an injustice to any person, the following royal order was issued against me.

"1st February, 1775.

"The Chevalier de Pontgibaud, *being of a fierce and violent character, and refusing to do work of any kind,* is to be taken to Saint Lazare, at the expense of his father."

But in the margin of the royal order,—which I have seen in the register preserved in the archives,—is written, "Transferred to Pierre-en-Cize, 19th February, 1775." It is clear also, from the date, that the *lettre de cachet* must have been signed "La Vrillière," for his successor, M. de Malesherbes, would certainly have refused to put his name to it. *

Where were human justice, a father's wisdom, the voice of nature, and the ties of blood? And yet I can honestly aver that my relatives, who all belonged to a high rank of society, were the best meaning people in the world,—all gentleness, and kindness,—though, perhaps, I should add, except towards me, and except on that occasion. That was the sad effect of prejudice. If you have respectable, well-to-do people for your judges, they may be mistaken like anyone else; and their judgments are severe, and not always just.

Accordingly you see that, on the sole charge of having,—at sixteen,—" a fierce and violent character, and refusing to do any kind of work," I found myself on the 19th February, 1775, on the road from Paris to Lyon, or, more strictly speaking, on the road to Pierre-en-Cize. The child had by his side his nurse,—I mean a gendarme,—and before him the pleasant prospect of remaining locked up for the remainder of his life.

* De Malesherbes never issued an order unless good cause was shown, and released many of the persons who had been imprisoned by his predecessors. He had, at the date given, been Minister for the last three months, but being busily engaged in putting to rights the State finances, was probably unable to look after other affairs. The Duc de La Vrillière allowed his mistress to do quite an extensive business in *lettres de cachet*, and she would sell a *blank form* (which the purchaser could fill in according to taste) for 50 louis.

CHAPTER II.

Eighteen months in prison—A plan of escape successfully carried out—Armed resistance—Sheltered by a Lyons merchant—Arrival in Auvergne—A family compact—A compromise effected—Departure to join the, so-called, "insurgent army" in America.

IN order that the intelligent reader may follow my narrative with interest, it is indispensable that I should here describe the castle of Pierre-en-Cize, the residence that I had taken on a long lease, or rather for an indefinite period, and of which I was an unwilling tenant. I must first though say something of the locality.

In Piganiol de la Force (see his *Description of France*) we find: "Pierre-en-Cize, or Pierre-Scise, a castle of France, and a State prison, near the Saône, and opposite Lyon. There are in this castle a captain on half pay, a company of thirty infantry soldiers, a lieutenant, and a sergeant."

That is all that a historian, a traveller, and a poet, could say about Pierre-en-Cize,—not having had an opportunity of examining the place closely. To properly describe the castle, one ought to have lived there, and been a State prisoner there, as I have been, but I do not think it likely that anyone will envy me my knowledge, considering how it was attained.

The castle of Pierre-en-Cize was the country house of the Archbishops of Lyon, and as far as situation and outlook are concerned, is a pleasant residence enough. It is not like the castle of Lourdes, surrounded by cloud-capped peaks, resembling a solitary cypress tree in a chaos of rocks, a veritable battle-field of the Titans. It is not like Mont St. Michel either, where, half the year, every twelve hours, the waves beat against the walls of your prison, the tempests roll under your feet, and the cry of the shipwrecked sailors echoes through the cells. Without prejudice, I may say that, as far as the view goes, Pierre-en-Cize is infinitely more pleasant, but there is no such thing as a nice prison, and, all things considered, it must be owned that,—when one is behind the bars,—the smiling fields, the harvests, the forests, the flocks, the sight of men at liberty, though they make a delightful picture, are only an added punishment to the poor prisoner.

Let me now give in my own fashion, and according to my own observations, a topographical and picturesque description of Pierre-en-Cize, internally and externally. It may be confidently accepted as correct, for I may say with truth, "I have seen."

The castle is situated on the banks of the Saône, as you enter Lyon by the *faubourg* of Vaize. It stands on a high and steep hill, which you ascend by steps cut in the rock. At the main-gate is a guard-house, occupied by a company of the Lyonnais regiment,— some of them veterans, but a good number young soldiers of good conduct, admitted into the garrison as a favour. There was no possible means of escape this way; moreover, the prisoners were only allowed to walk in a portion of the courtyard; the sentinel stopped them if they passed the boundary,—a big chestnut tree, which I can still see in my mind's eye.

The castle is a square building, having at the north-west corner a very large tower, at the end of the courtyard on the right hand side. All the walls are very high; that part of the castle which looks towards the *faubourg* of Vaize is to the north-east, and is only accessible on that side by a road cut in the hill for the purpose of bringing up wood, wine, and other provisions and necessaries, which are all brought on the backs of mules. Whenever anything of this kind arrives, the entire guard turns out under arms, and, as long as the gates are open, half the soldiers stand outside, and the other half just inside, the gateway. But by observing as much as I could, I was able to form some idea as to the nature of the ground on that side, which had hitherto been unknown to me, I having arrived by the gate which overlooks the river Saône, by which, as I have said before, escape was impossible.

After having mounted the rock, I was conducted

through the courtyard, and found myself at the foot of the great tower, the situation of which I have already described. I was led up a winding staircase to a wooden gallery, and locked in cell No. 1, close to the tower, the circular wall of which formed one side of my cell. I found, in this agreeable abode, the regulation prison-furniture; a wretched bed, pushed against the rounded wall of the tower, a chair, a table, and the usual big jar of water. Light came from the inside court, through a window well garnished with bars, and looking on the gallery. Such was my prison, and such were the obstacles I should have to surmount in order to get out of it, but I had no sooner put my foot inside the tower than I resolved to attempt to make my escape, and that as soon as I possibly could. The contrivance, the patience, the hard work, and the boldness of my escape, which I made in full daylight, and with arms in my hand, rendered me somewhat celebrated in the history of Pierre-en-Cize. The castle was destroyed in the Revolution (in 1791), but it is a fact that from 1777 till the time the fortress was demolished, every young prisoner who was confined there longed to emulate the prowess of Pontgibaud. It will be seen that for a prisoner, aged only eighteen, to make his escape is a feat of which I may be allowed to boast.

No pupil of Vauban ever made more calculations and plans how to get into a stronghold than I did how to get out of mine. I said to myself, "This castle is accessible on the side where I am. I ought to be able to cut through the wall where it joins the tower. The wall and the tower were built at different times, and though the facings are in hard stone, there is sure to be only rubble between,—more particularly in the angle where the straight wall joins the round tower. All that is needed is time and patience, and that I will have."

The prisoner who had occupied the cell before me had a talent for painting, and a taste for botany. He had amused himself by painting all sorts of flowers on the walls, and, which was greatly in my favour, he had painted a dark blue border, about two and a half feet high, all round the room. I may note also as a strange freak of chance, that this predecessor was a near relative of my aunt. I will not say that she had anything to do with his imprisonment, for I never inquired the reason of it, but at any rate it caused the cell to seem quite like a family apartment. The purchase of a quantity of blue paper,—the paper in which hair powder is usually packed,—was therefore one of my first steps, for the sapper required a mantlet behind which he could work. Above all, I had need of money. Money has been called the sinews of war, and is certainly necessary in all great enterprises, and no enterprise was greater in my eyes than that which absorbed all my thoughts. Virgil has said,

> Quid non mortalia pectora cogis
> Auri sacra fames.

If he had been in my place he would have said, as I did, *sacra fames libertatis*.

I received fifty francs a month, to enable me to supplement my scanty fare with better food, and hire books. I found means to augment this scanty income by copying music in the daytime. The Amphions of Lyon had many a score from my hand, and I had their money; they were, without knowing it, half accomplices in my escape. I procured some cardboard, with which I made shutters to my window, because at ten o'clock the sentinel ordered us to put out our lights. I bought, under various pretexts, some small knives, and as we were supplied with wood for the winter, I manufactured out of the largest faggots, short levers intended to make an opening through the wall, without any noise, by working with them between the stones. I also procured, through the help of my laundress, some bullets, gunpowder, and a double-barrelled pistol. Trust in women, and you will never have cause to repent it. If they consent to help you, they will never betray you, and they will keep your secret as they would keep their own. This is not always the case with men. If there is cited against me the mother of Papirius Praetextatus, I will reply with the name of Epicharis *; and as regards men my worthy laundress was more discreet than Turenne.

---

* Epicharis, a freed woman of bad repute, who conspired against Nero. When the plot was discovered she was horribly tortured but would not reveal the names of her accomplices. She strangled herself with her girdle

I had now nothing to do but set to work. The
angle made by the wall and the tower was concealed by my bed. I commenced to tunnel at this
spot, taking care not to surpass the limit of the
blue paint. My paper, which was of the same
colour, covered and concealed my sapping. I
worked four hours every night. I was careful to
sweep away all signs of work, and to neatly re-
place the blue paper before my "gate of safety."
As to the rubbish I took out, I carefully carried it
in handkerchiefs, and easily disposed of it by throwing it down the latrine used by the prisoners. This
was at the foot of the staircase inside the tower.
My cell was No. 1, and being so close to the stairs,
I could descend twenty times a day without being
noticed, and, by a lucky chance also, the cesspool
was a sort of well of great depth.

My labour was greatly lessened by the fact that
the wall,—as I had hoped,—did not join the tower
in the centre, there was a gap of two or there
inches; and throughout the whole of my labours,
in digging through a wall nine or ten feet thick,
I only met with one very large stone. It caused
me some disappointment, and led me to take counsel
with myself. This huge stone presented an acute
angle towards me. I attacked the wall round it,
but with no great hope of success. Judge of my

---

to escape further torture. The "mother of Praetextatus" is, I suppose,
the person mentioned in Livy VI.. 32—38, but if so the comparison is
not well chosen. ED.

joy and surprise when I felt it yield under my poor little lever, like a loose tooth. I soon had the happiness to lay it bare, and then drag it out of my mole-run. I did not think of breaking it up, but hid it, as it was, in my mattress. It was found there later on, and figured in the report on my escape; but it did not tend to make my bed feel any the more comfortable. The first part of the work was the most difficult, because the nine or ten inches of plaster I had to get though, prevented my seeing the real positions of the stones, which I had then to attack very warily for fear that they should bring down with them, when they fell, some of the plaster above the line of blue paint. I made my tunnel so that, when I had crawled in on my stomach, I could then draw up my legs, and sit like a journeyman tailor. The light to work by, I obtained in the best way I could, by converting pomade pots into lamps, filling them with lard, and inserting a bit of wick.

The "solution of continuity," existing between the wall and the tower, allowed me to respire the external air, which was a great relief to me. I calculated that I had still nearly four feet of masonry to cut through, and that I was about half through my work, when, about eleven o'clock or midnight, I heard a voice pronounce these terrible words:

"Look, papa, there is a light at the foot of the castle tower."

The words were uttered by a little boy, the son

of the gardener. My blood ran cold; I put my hand over my little lamp, but the burn and the fright were the worst that was to happen to me. The worthy man thought that the child was mistaken, and so I was saved.

The work was at last finished;—it had occupied me forty-five nights. What thoughts crowded in upon me. This wall ten feet thick was now nothing for me but a thin partition of a few inches; with a kick, or a push with my shoulder, I could throw down the feeble barrier which separated me from the world and from liberty. But then what should I do when I was free? I was without means,—for I had but six francs in my pocket. Then, should I make my escape alone? Would it not be more honourable to set at liberty all my companions in misfortune, as well as myself. They must be all innocent, for they said they were. What a debt they would owe me for the rest of their lives, and besides, if we were attacked we should be able to defend ourselves.

I resolved on adopting this noble idea, but I would say nothing beforehand,—for fear I should be betrayed.

I suspended my labours the following day, and when we re-entered the castle to be locked up in our several cells, I told five or six of the prisoners to come to No. 1 as soon as the doors were opened in the morning, and I would inform them of a certain means of escape.

I could not get them all out at night; it would be necessary to break through all the walls which separated the cells, with all the chances of being discovered or betrayed, but the regulations of the prison greatly favoured another plan.

Our cell doors were opened at precisely seven o'clock every morning, and our food was brought to us at ten; thus there were three hours during which nobody paid any attention to us.

The night before the projected attempt it was impossible for me to close my eyes, with such inquietude and impatience did I await the appointed hour. I will even confess that several times I was tempted to make my escape alone, but I resisted the thought. When the breach was opened, I did not know what height I should have to descend, therefore, during the night, I cut up my sheets and linen to make a rope if necessary.

At last the hour struck, the lock turned, and the gaoler entered, and wished me good day, as usual. My five comrades soon appeared; one of them said to me, in a mocking voice,

"Well, let us know this fine plan."

"The plan," I replied, "is in this corner, behind this wall—which is only paper. Let us make haste."

"Is it possible?" they cried.

"He found this hole ready made.—It is not finished. What is there gained by that?"

"It is not finished—but it can be with a single push.—Let those who love me follow me."

We fastened my sheets to the leg of my bed; I took the end of this hastily devised cord, and entered the narrow passage. I was in a nankeen vest, and had in my pockets six cartridges, a double-barrelled pistol, and a strong "spring-back" knife. I cannot describe my emotion. I trembled all over with hope and fear. Someone behind me cried, "Make haste." In a few moments I had pushed down the wall, which was only a thin partition of stones, but the opening was so narrow that two or three minutes,— which seemed to my impatience like two or three centuries, for there was not a moment to lose,— elapsed before I could get my shoulders free. At the sound of the stones rattling down, the gardener, who was at work below, ran to his cottage, built against the castle wall, and rang the alarm bell. The guard turned out, and took up their position on the very spot I should have to pass, for it would take me eight or ten minutes to descend to the foot of the tower, and I should then find myself between the castle gates and the soldiers.

One prisoner alone, M. de L——, dared to follow me,—the others recoiled at the sight of danger,— but my comrade was only armed with a broomstick pointed at both ends. The tocsin sounded, and all the windows which looked out on this side of the castle were filled with spectators. The major commanding the castle came running out in his drawers, and with bare legs, and crying, "Load your arms!" He ordered me to go back, and threatened that I should be fired on if I did not. My only reply was to present my pistol, and order him to go back himself.

The major ran away, crying, "Fire on the scoundrels!" I fancy I can still see the old sergeant, who was a friend of mine, his musket levelled, but trembling in his hands, and hear him beg of me to go back. I took no notice; we were at fifteen paces from each other. I advanced boldly—ten or twelve muskets went off at the same moment;—I replied with a single shot and charged furiously into the midst of them. I heard on all sides cries of "Bravo! Bravo!" and applause at the windows. I was assailed with the butts of muskets, and received blows of which my ribs showed the marks for long afterwards; my vest was nearly torn off, and my hair pulled out. My poor comrade De L—— was wounded and thrown down, after having knocked out the eye of one of the soldiers, and bitten the finger of another;—they all threw themselves upon him, and—I was saved.

Incidit in Scyllam,—I was in a narrow lane between two walls, which I did not dare to leap, being closely pursued by the youngest soldiers of the troop, who were crying behind me, "Stop! Stop!" I presented my weapon at all who tried to bar my passage, and received more bows and salutes than I have ever had either before or since. The road, which was tortuous, was nearly a quarter of a league long, or at least seemed so to me. Hearing no more cries of "Stop! Stop!" I rested for a few minutes, and reloaded my pistol, when all of a sudden there appeared within ten paces of me, four soldiers who had pursued me for the sake of the reward. I put my back against the wall, and they stopped short.

"Well, sir," said one of them, "you see you are caught,—you can't go any further. It was good of you to try to save all the others;—if they had all been as brave as you they would have succeeded, but they were cowards. Come back, sir; you run no risk, and your relations will soon take you out of prison. Besides, *you* haven't hurt anybody; it was the Marquis de L—— who wounded two of our men."

I listened quietly till they had finished, for I wanted to regain my breath. Then I replied,

"Go away! I don't want to hurt you, but I swear that I will never be taken alive. There are four of you, and I can rely on killing at least two." And with that I held out my pistol in one hand, and my knife in the other.

They looked at me a minute, and then one said,

"Good-bye. You are a brave young fellow. A pleasant journey, and good luck to you;" and they went away.

I also ran off, but without exactly knowing where I was going. The clang of the alarm bell, and the firing, had already caused rumours to be in circulation about me, and the name of the prisoner, and his bold escape, were known in Vaize.

Women came to their doors, and cried, "Come in, sir, and we will conceal you." But I had no intention of stopping; I was too near the terrible prison, and I ran away faster than ever, but the voices of these women sank into my soul; though I had not had time to glance at one of them, I fancied that every woman who had offered to conceal me must be beautiful,—for did she not feel for my distresses, and wish to relieve them?

Marcelines, Suzannes, Comtesse Almavivas, I saw you all,—mentally; and I would have kissed you all,—but I had no time.

The houses began to get fewer and fewer, as I ran on, and at last I came to a small copse of trees and thick underwood, which would afford me a refuge. In the centre was a grass-plot a few yards square, and my first act was to throw myself on the grass and take some rest.

Profound silence reigned all round; I enjoyed the delightful sensation of breathing the pure air of liberty, of which I had been so long deprived. In the midst of all my thoughts, the ruling idea was pride. I thought that my escape would give me some notoriety, and perhaps be useful to me in the future, if I should adopt the military profession; but my thoughts then reverted to the question of the moment, what should I do? I did not know where I was; my only coat was a thin nankeen, badly torn in my fight, I had no hat, and my legs were bleeding from the thorns amidst which

I had fallen when I descended the tower. What with my rags covered with blood, and my wild, haggard appearance, I must have looked like a poor devil who had been in the wars, and not got the best of it. My good angel, however, directed me to a respectable-looking house at a little distance, and I saw, walking in front of it, a person whom I imagined to be the proprietor. It was then about nine o'clock in the morning, and as it was July, the weather was very warm. I made up my mind on the spot, and advanced towards this unknown personage, who, luckily for me, turned out to be one of the best-natured men in the world—a M. Bontems, a merchant, of the Rue Mercière, Lyon. I have since been happy to acknowledge and repay the service he rendered me.

He did not see me till I was within eight or ten yards of him. He was a good-looking man, with a florid complexion, but at the sight of me he became deadly pale, and trembled. He kept his eyes fixed on the butt of the pistol, which was sticking out of my pocket, and stood motionless without the power to say a word.

"Pray be easy, my good sir," I said, "and listen to what I have to say. Never mind the horrible condition in which I am. I am the happiest man in the world, for I have just acquired my liberty; the alarm bell which is ringing up there, and which you can hear distinctly, is sounding on my account. I have got out of Pierre-en-Cize, and my body must be as black as a negro's from the blows I received in my fight with the castle guard. This house belongs to you, I suppose. Give me shelter till nightfall, for I am worn out with fatigue and hunger. I would hand over to you this minute the weapon which so much terrifies you, if I did not fear to be surprised without any means of defence. If you are humane enough to take me in, show me some way of getting into the house without being perceived."

The worthy man was touched by my address, and the trust I reposed in him, and showed me a way through his garden by which I could enter the house without being seen by anyone. M. Bontems led me into a room on the ground floor, where his old mother was sitting. She was quite as frightened as her son, but began to weep when I recounted my adventures. They brought me some refreshments, of which I had sore need.

My host meanwhile took the very natural precaution of sending to Lyon, and the neighbourhood of the castle, to know why the alarm bell was ringing. My statements were confirmed, and everybody was speaking highly of me, because I had nearly fallen a victim to my own generosity in endeavouring to set the other prisoners at liberty. M. Bontems, being perfectly satisfied as to the truth of my story, offered to be of service to me in any way. He wished to conceal me in his house, but I would not accept this kindness. I asked him only to furnish me with some clothes and a hat, and procure me a horse, and a guide, so that I might start that night by the old Lyon road, which is little frequented, and by which I could get home to my father's house,—a distance of but thirty leagues. M. Bontems procured me all I asked, and supplied me with the money necessary for my journey. You may imagine my affection and gratitude, when I said farewell to this worthy man and his good old mother.

I left this hospitable roof, and made my way towards Clermont.

The future was before me. I did not look back, for I should have seen that cursed castle, the very recollection of which made me shiver, for past dangers make more impression on the mind than present perils. Except for some vague misgivings, which I could not prevent, I made the journey peaceably enough, but I reflected that as my father would not expect to see me, there was a risk that my sudden appearance would give him a shock, which, considering his great age, might be dangerous, and for which I should always reproach myself. I thought it wise, therefore, to stop at the house of a friend of our family, who lived two leagues from Pontgibaud. When I arrived at the Château d'A——, there was a large gathering of friends and visitors. My adventures were not yet known to anyone in Auvergne. It was as though I fell from the clouds, for certainly no one expected me, for all knew that

I was in Pierre-en-Cize, though my poor old father sometimes asked himself why I was there.

It was a really dramatic situation; the servants—almost a second family in the distant parts of the country—surrounded me, and I arrived in the *salon* in the midst of them. It was crowded with people who all began to ask questions, and I did not know what to reply to all these men and women, young and old. Some laughed at my dress, some of the women cried when they heard my story, and all were interested in it. It was quite a picture: I felt like Telemachus relating his adventures in the cave of Calypso, but with the difference that there was nothing fabulous in my story. All the neighbours, men as well as women, masters as well as servants, had tears in their eyes, for at that time French people had not learned,—as they did later, in the school of the Revolution,— how to harden their hearts to distress.

All approved of my foresight in not presenting myself to my father until he had been prepared for my coming, and the master of the house undertook that duty. A welcome proposal was also made to me the same evening. I learned that England was at war with her American colonies; I heard also that the Marquis de la Fayette, who belonged to our province, had already made himself talked about, and it was suggested that it would be a good thing for me to join him and fight under his orders. I snapped at the idea enthusiastically, and my ambassador went to arrange the matter with my father.

M. d'A—— presented himself, let out the story by degrees, and made his old friend acquainted with all my adventures down to the minutest detail. There is generally a touch of the ludicrous, even in the gravest affairs. The aged author of my being listened very quietly to the history of my almost incredibly bold escape. He was no doubt struck by the difference in character between my brother, "the good young man," and me, "the bad lot," and remembering his young days when he was a musketeer, he said, with a smile,

"Ah, the rascal! Well, my friend, I'll tell you what it is. If I had locked up my elder son, instead of my younger,—he would have stopped there for ever."

Peace was concluded, and all the conditions were granted, with one exception. My father steadfastly refused to see me;—not that he was angry with me, for his wrath had completely disappeared, but from quite another motive. He was an old soldier, and knew the rules of the service. He remarked that I had fired upon the King's soldiers, which might get me into trouble, and he did not wish to be exposed to the unpleasantness of seeing the gendarmes visit the château to search for me.

It was decided that I should start for North America; that my father should make me an allowance of 100 louis a year; and that 2000 crowns should be counted down to me at the port where I embarked.

I left at once for La Rochelle, with a letter of recommendation to M. Seigneur, *commissaire* of artillery.

It might have been expected that I should obtain a passage without any difficulty, but I was obliged to go to Nantes. Only two days after my arrival at La Rochelle, orders were received by the military commander, Baron de M——, to arrest me. What a debt of gratitude do I owe him! He was kind enough to cause a hint to be conveyed to M. Seigneur to get me out of the way.

I left therefore for Nantes with a letter of recommendation from M. Seigneur to M. de Ville-Hélis, the government outfitter. I shall always remember the hearty welcome he gave me. He kindly interested himself in all the details of my situation; gave me some excellent advice how to lay out my money, and the means to augment my resources by the purchase of goods likely to be required in the country to which I was going. Finally, he procured—and at a very low rate—a passage on the ship *Arc-en-Ciel*, fitted out by Messrs. Minier and Struckman, and recommended me to the care of the captain. And so I sailed for the New World.

CHAPTER III.

Wrecked in Chesapeake Bay—Williamsburg—Mr. Jefferson—Aspect of the country between Williamsburg and the Camp at Valley Forges—Description of the American Army—Welcomed by Marquis de la Fayette—He appoints me his aide-de-camp—My mission to the Oneida Indians—American ideas of the French—The Camp at Valley Forges—General Howe's dog—Attempted sortie of the British Army from Philadelphia—The passage of the Schuylkill and return—Our ambulance surgeon—Evacuation of Philadelphia—Defeat at Rareton Rivers—Battle and Victory at Monmouth—New York blockaded—Arnold's treason—Arrest, trial, and execution of Major André—The Earl of Carlisle and Marquis de la Fayette—Comte d'Estaing before New York—Siege of Newport, Rhode Island, by Gen. Sullivan—I am charged with the re-victualling of the French fleet—The siege of Newport raised—Our departure for France on board the frigate "Alliance"—A storm and its consequences—Mutiny on board—Capture of a British cruiser—Arrival at Brest.

OUR voyage, which was a very bad one, lasted sixty-seven days. We met with a heavy storm off the Bermudas, and were often chased by British cruisers. At last we came in sight of Capes Charles and Henry at the entrance to Chesapeake Bay.

As it was then almost night-fall the captain tacked

about, intending to enter the Bay next morning. We then had a good wind behind us, and we hoped, but in vain, for a pilot to come off and take us in. The fear of being captured, however, made the captain determine to enter the Bay, which is very large. The destination of the vessel was Baltimore, but we were obliged to run into James River. The morning was very foggy, and we could not see more than a hundred yards or so. A few minutes later the fog lifted, the sun came out, and we found ourselves within a couple of cannon shot of the *Isis*, a British war vessel of 64 guns, which was moored at the entrance to the river. We might have run ashore on the coast, and the *Isis* could not have come near us as the wind was against her, but our captain lost his head and gave no orders, so we drifted within range of the *Isis*, and then went aground near the shore. The British being now convinced we were enemies, began to fire on us.

All the shore pirates of the district at once embarked to pillage us, and a scene of terrible disorder ensued. These sea wolves, nearly all negroes or mulattos, and numbering, as near as I could guess, about sixty, came on board under the pretext of saving the vessel, but they cared more for pillage than salvage, for they staved in casks of wine and brandy, and the greater part of them were soon very drunk. I noticed that their boats were secured to the ship by thin cords, so I quickly engaged a boy and one of our sailors to help me to bring up from the cabin my trunk which contained my goods, —alas! all my fortune,--and my other effects. We threw these into a boat belonging to one of the Lestrigons, whilst the owner was engaged in drinking and stealing, then we jumped in ourselves, cut the rope, and in a very few minutes were on shore.

The bullets whistled over our heads, but we were safe, and I had, moreover (as I thought), preserved all my property. Seated on my trunk, with my feet on the shore of America, I watched the total destruction of our ship, which was accomplished in a very few hours. We did not know what to do, or where to go, for we could not tell in which direction any houses lay. We could not speak the language, and we could not see any of the inhabitants of the country. At last several of the boats belonging to the robbers arrived, loaded with booty taken from the ship. Some of our sailors were in the boats. The leader of the pirates sent to the neighbouring town of Hampton for wagons, and when they came packed in them all which had been brought to shore, including my trunk and all that belonged to the passengers. I heard, however, the words, "Public Magazine," and that reassured me a little, for I imagined that when all the passengers were assembled, each would be allowed to claim and take away his own property.

In two or three days the crew got together, except two killed, and one or two drowned, and the doors of the Public Magazine were opened for us. My eyes filled with joy at again beholding the trunk which contained all my riches. The key was in my pocket; I approached my trunk, but, alas! found that the padlock had been broken off, the lock forced, and, instead of the fine Dutch linen upon which I expected to make such a profit, I found only sail covers, stones, and a few rags of sails.

You may imagine my distress. I was thousands of miles from home, with no property except the clothes on my back, and no money except the nine or ten louis I chanced to have in my pocket.

Being weak and fatigued by the long voyage and its exciting incidents, I rested for a day or two, but not wishing to expend all my slender stock of money in an inn at Hampton, I set off to join the army, and, in order to get information, I first directed my steps towards Williamsburg, the capital of Virginia, about twenty or twenty-five miles distant from my starting point.

I was sure that, when once I had joined the army, I should run no risk by dying of hunger at all events; but it was a long way to the camp, and I did not know within a trifling matter of a hundred miles or so, where the head-quarters then were. Besides there were forests to pass through, and I was not sure whether I might not meet with bears, panthers, or rattlesnakes—at least that was what I had to expect if I believed all the books of travel I had read whilst I was in prison. I foresaw that I should often have to sleep under the stars, which, in the month of November, is neither safe nor pleasant in any country remote from the equator, and I was also doubtful as to whether I should find a dinner every day. With thoughts like these, but with no anxiety as to my baggage, I started off on the road—which was only a worn path—to Williamsburg.

There I found some Frenchmen, for they are to be met with everywhere. They provided me with a map of the country and I planned out my route. I learned that the army was camped at Valley Forges, three leagues from Philadelphia, and that there I should find the Marquis de la Fayette. It was a long journey to make on foot. I related the story of my shipwreck on the coast of Chesapeake Bay, and, as advice costs nothing, everybody was ready to give it, and all recommended me to complain to Mr. Jefferson, then governor of Virginia, of the robbery of my effects.

After my experience in the Old World, and more recent vicissitudes in the New, I was not inclined to be too hopeful, but, to ease my mind, I called on the governor, accompanied by an interpreter. I found that Mr. Jefferson had been informed of our misfortunes. He expressed his regret that in such troublous times as we were then in, it was impossible for him to pay me the compensation to which I was entitled. In my presence he ordered his secretary to give me a certificate. This curious document was in English, which I could neither speak nor read, but later on I was able to peruse the document. The governor terminated his passport by recommending me to the charity of all with whom I might meet!

What freaks fortune had played with me. At nineteen years of age I had escaped from Pierre-en-Cize,—two months later had been shipwrecked a thousand leagues from home,—had been robbed of all I possessed, on a friendly shore, by the very persons I had come to help to regain their liberty,—and now I was trudging on foot to the head-quarters of the army, the bearer of a licence to beg on the road. Fortunately the little money I had sufficed, and I was not obliged to take advantage of the charitable verb "to assist", slipped in for my special benefit at the foot of the passport.

From Williamsburg to the camp at Valley Forges, near Philadelphia, is not less than 200 miles, and it must not be supposed that it required any superhuman effort to accomplish that. There was plenty of mud to be found—but that I expected; the weather was not always fine, for it rained often—in the months of November and December it rains even in France. In the midst of all these discomforts, which I foresaw would have an end, the knowledge that I was free sustained me, and comforted me. Moreover, I was young, and had health and strength. It is not astonishing therefore that I found at every step something fresh to drive away sad thoughts.

Birds unknown in France enlivened my view, and made me admire the richness and variety of their plumage, and in the almost continuous forest through which I had to pass, I was never tired of watching the thousands of little squirrels which leaped from bough to bough and tree to tree round me.

My baggage consisted of a single shirt. I had in my pocket a flask which I filled with gin (whenever I could get it) and in another pocket a hunk of bad maize bread. I had also five louis in my purse and a passport, signed "Jefferson."

Sand and forest, forest and sand, formed the whole way from Williamsburg to the camp at Valley Forges. I do not remember how many days I took to accomplish this difficult journey. Being badly fed, as a natural consequence I walked badly, and passed at least six nights under the trees through not meeting with any habitation. Not knowing the language, I often strayed from the right road, which was so much time and labour lost. At last, early in November, I arrived at Valley Forges.

The American army was then encamped three or four leagues from Philadelphia, which city was then occupied by the British, who were rapidly fulfilling the prophecy of Dr. Franklin.

That celebrated man—an ambassador who amused himself with science, which he adroitly made to assist him in his diplomatic work—said, when some friends came to Passy to condole with him on the fall of Philadelphia, "You are mistaken; it is not the British army that has taken Philadelphia, but Philadelphia that has taken the British army." The cunning old diplomatist was right. The capital of Pennsylvania had already done for the British what Capua did in a few months for the soldiers of Hannibal. The Americans,—the "insurgents" as they were called,—camped at Valley Forges; the British officers, who were in the city, gave themselves up to pleasure, there were continual balls and other amusements; the troops were idle and enervated by inaction, and the generals undertook nothing all the winter.

Soon I came in sight of the camp. My imagination had pictured an army with uniforms, the glitter of arms, standards, etc., in short, military pomp of all sorts. Instead of the imposing spectacle I expected, I saw, grouped together or standing alone, a few militia men, poorly clad, and for the most part without shoes;—many of them badly armed, but all well supplied with provisions, and I noticed that tea and sugar formed part of their rations. I did not then know that this was not unusual, and I laughed, for it made me think of the recruiting sergeants on the Quai de la Ferraille at Paris, who say to the yokels, "You will want for nothing when you are in the regiment, but if bread should run short you must not mind eating cakes." Here the soldiers had tea and sugar. In passing through the camp I also noticed soldiers wearing cotton night-caps under their hats, and some having for cloaks or great-coats, coarse woollen blankets, exactly like those provided for the patients in our French hospitals. I learned afterwards that these were the officers and generals.

Such, in strict truth, was,—at the time I came amongst them,—the appearance of this armed mob, the leader of whom was the man who has rendered the name of Washington famous; such were the colonists,—unskilled warriors who learned in a few years how to conquer the finest troops that England could send against them. Such also,—at the beginning of the War of Independence,—was the state of want in the insurgent army, and such was the scarcity of money, and the poverty of that government, now so rich, powerful, and prosperous, that its notes, called Continental Paper Money, were nearly valueless, like our own assignats in 1795.

Impressed by these sights, which had quite destroyed my illusions, I made my way through this singular army to the quarters of Marquis de la Fayette.

This young general was then, I believe, not more than 20 or 21 years of age. I presented myself to him, and told him frankly my whole story. He listened to my history with attention and kindness, and at my request enrolled me as a volunteer. He also wrote to France and before long received a reply confirming the truth of my statements; he then appointed me one of his *aides-de-camp*, with the rank of Major, and from that moment never ceased to load me with benefits and marks of confidence. The Marquis de la Fayette presented me as his *aide-de-camp* to the commander-in-chief. Washington was intended by nature for a great position,—his appearance alone gave confidence to the timid, and imposed respect on the bold. He possessed also those external advantages which a man born to command should have; tall stature, a noble face, gentleness in his glance, amenity in his language, simplicity in his gestures and expressions. A calm, firm bearing harmonized perfectly with these attributes. This general, who has since become so celebrated for his talents and successes, was just beginning to play that important part in history that he has since so gloriously sustained, in every capacity, military, civil, and political. But I intend here only to speak of the general.

He was surrounded by his officers, who for the most part were, like me, on their first campaign. Many of them had been far from imagining, a short time before, that they were intended for a military career. I saw, standing near the Commander in Chief, Gates, the victor at Saratoga, a small man, about fifty years of age: two years before that he was merely a rich farmer, yet quiet and simple as he looked he had made himself a name in history. This agriculturist turned soldier, who was wearing on his head a woollen cap surmounted by a farmer's hat, had just received the sword of General Burgoyne, who, dressed in full uniform, and with his breast covered with all the orders England could give, came to him to surrender.

Near Gates was Arnold, as brave as he was treacherous; he was lamed for life by a bullet he had received at Saratoga whilst sharing the dangers and glories of General Gates. A few months before he was a distinguished officer in the army, General Arnold was nothing more than a horse-dealer. General Lee, however, was a soldier before the War of Independence. General Sullivan was a lawyer, and when peace was declared he returned, not to his plough but to his office. Colonel Hamilton, the friend of Washington, when the war was over, also became a lawyer, and pleaded at Philadelphia. General Stark was the proprietor of a large and well-managed estate. Brave General Knox, who commanded the artillery, had, before the war, kept a book-store. Under him served Duplessis-Mauduit, a brave young officer, only twenty-six years old, and of whom I shall often have occasion to speak in these pages;—he afterwards perished at Saint-Domingo, vilely murdered by his own soldiers.

I also saw arrive at the mill which served our commander as his head-quarters, Colonel Armand, then commanding a troop of light horse. The life of this young Frenchman, who was then twenty-four, had been like mine, adventurous from the beginning. He was the nephew of the Marquis de la Beliniese, and had been an officer in the Gardes Françaises. Having fallen madly in love with Mlle Beaumesnil, of the Opera, and been refused by her, he retired to the Monastery of La Trappe, which he left to seek danger by the side of General Washington. He had earned some glory and distinction under the name of Colonel Armand, and was to become more celebrated under the name of the Marquis de la Rouarie.

Lastly I saw there, for the first time, Monsieur de P——,* who commanded the Engineers, and who was afterwards Minister of War to Louis XVI, at the beginning of the Revolution.

Amongst all these officers of different nationalities and habits I noticed more particularly the striking figure of the man before whom all bowed, as much from admiration and respect as from duty. General Washington appeared to be about forty. He had served in the British army, and as Major Washington commanded in 175— Fort Necessity, when M. de Jumonville, a French officer bearing a flag of truce, was shot by a private soldier, who did not see the white flag, and who fired without orders. According to all reports it is certain that the commander of the fort never gave any order to fire, and the most irrefutable proof of this is the gentleness, magnanimity, and goodness of General Washington,— a character which he never once belied amidst all the chances of war, and all the trials of good or

* See Note B.

bad fortune. M. Thomas * has deemed it proper and patriotic to paint this unfortunate occurrence in the worst light, and severely blame the British officer. Had the name of Major Washington remained obscure, it would have been stained with an undeserved blot which no one would have thought it worth while to remove, but, as it is, any attempt to answer the charge would be an insult to one of the most beautiful and noble characters in history, and all suspicions fall to the ground before the name, the virtues, and the glory of General Washington. The assassin of De Jumonville could never have become a great man.

When the war broke out, General Washington was the proprietor of a splendid estate in Virginia, and he brought with him when he joined the army, a number of fine horses. He dressed in the most simple manner, without any of the marks distinctive of a commanding officer, and he gave away large sums to the soldiers, by whom he was adored. But all that he gave was from his own purse, for he had refused to receive any emoluments from the Government.

I ought to mention to the praise of the Marquis de la Fayette, that he followed the example of the commander-in-chief, and incurred great expense, purchasing with his own money all that was necessary to clothe, equip, and arm his men. The war cost him immense sums, and certainly no one will

* See Note C.

suspect him of any other motive than the noble one of glory, for the chances of reimbursement were not very probable. His motives were perfectly pure, and the enormous sacrifices he made can only be accounted for by the love of liberty, and the chivalric spirit which will always exist in France;—enthusiasm, love of danger, and a little glory were his sole rewards. The pleasure of commanding, fighting, and distinguishing himself were of some weight in the scale, it is reasonable to conclude, but honour and merit were the principal motives. The war in America only offered a chance of danger, privations, fatigues, and difficulties; the Marquis de la Fayette was the only one of all the young lords of the Court of France who had the courage and determination to leave the pleasures of the palace, and travel eighteen hundred leagues to obtain glory without profit.

Moreover, there was not an opportunity every day of acquiring even this much, under General Washington. It did not enter into his plans to readily engage with the enemy on every opportunity. He watched his time and chance before he struck a blow; the principle of "armed temporization" was his daily study; and, as events have proved, he well deserved the title which has been claimed for him of the American Fabius.

The British, occupied in the pleasures which they found in Philadelphia, allowed us to pass the winter in tranquillity; they never spoke of the camp at

Valley Forges except to joke about it, and we for our part might almost have forgotten that we were in the presence of an enemy if we had not received a chance visitor. We were at table at head-quarters,—that is to say in the mill, which was comfortable enough,—one 'day, when a fine sporting dog, which was evidently lost, came to ask for some dinner. On its collar were the words, *General Howe.* It was the British commander's dog. It was sent back under a flag of truce, and General Howe replied by a warm letter of thanks to this act of courtesy on the part of his enemy, our general.

When I arrived at the camp I was in a pitiable condition, but the Marquis de la Fayette had the extreme kindness to furnish me with the means of procuring horses and a suitable equipment.

A plan was proposed to effect a diversion by attacking Canada, where, we were informed, we should find few troops to oppose us, and towards the middle of January, the Marquis de la Fayette went to take command of the troops in the district round Albany.

We made the journey on sledges on the North River, and travelled with great speed, but the weather was "wickedly cold." One of our companions was the brave Duplessis-Mauduit, who was to command our artillery. But before undertaking any measures we thought it prudent to make a treaty with the savage races who live on the borders of Canada and New England.

After resting some days in the town of Albany, we went up Mohawk River to the house of Mr. Johnston whose residence was close to the huts of the various tribes known under the names of Tuscaroros, Oneidas, etc. We were prepared with the usual presents required to conciliate them, and in this case it might be said that little presents cement great friendships. Our gifts, which they thought magnificent, consisted of woollen blankets, little mirrors, and, above all, plenty of paint, which the savages esteem highly and use to paint their faces. There was also some gunpowder, lead, and bullets, and some silver crowns of six francs bearing the effigy of the King of France, who is known to these savages, by tradition, as the "Great Father."

About two thousand Indians, men and women, came to the appointed rendezvous, and thanks to our presents and the "fire water" which we distributed, the treaty was easily concluded. I was very anxious to observe the manners and customs of these people, who were a great novelty to me, but at the end of a few days I had seen quite enough, for the European beggar is far less disgusting than the American savage. Their numbers are diminishing rapidly from various causes.

We found amongst them an old soldier who had belonged to the Marquis de Montcalm's army. This man had become a savage; he had almost entirely forgotten French, and lived like the Indians, except that he had not let them cut his ears, which is the sign of a warrior. We left these tribes equally satisfied on both sides. The projected attack on Canada was postponed, for some reason of which I am ignorant, and we returned to the Camp at Valley Forges.

I remarked, however, that even in treating with these children of nature, there was a reciprocal distrust and an impression that caution was the mother of safety, for we brought with us fifty of the young warriors as a guarantee that the treaty should be duly executed, and one of our men remained with the Indians as a hostage—it was not I.

A little later some of these Indians joined our army, and I will here note two singular incidents concerning them. One day we were at dinner at head-quarters; an Indian entered the room, walked round the table, and then stretching forth his long tattooed arm seized a large joint of hot roast beef in his thumb and fingers, took it to the door, and began to eat it. We were all much surprised, but General Washington gave orders that he was not to be interfered with, saying laughingly, that it was apparently the dinner hour of this Mutius Scaevola of the New World.

On another occasion a chief came into the room where our generals were holding a council of war. Washington, who was tall and very strong, rose, coolly took the Indian by the shoulders, and put him outside the door. The son of the forest did not protest; he concluded probably that his ejectment was a way of expressing by signs that his company was not wanted.

At another time a meeting was appointed with the chiefs and warriors belonging to several tribes, which resided at great distances from each other in different directions. They had to pass through vast and thick forests where there were no paths. Though without either watch or compass they found their road, by means known to themselves alone. The meeting was to be on a plain, and it is a fact that on the day appointed we heard their songs and cries, and saw the various bodies of Indians arrive from all sides almost simultaneously.

I was astonished, on my return, to find what peculiar ideas our hosts, the Americans of New England, had of the French. One day I dismounted from my horse at the house of a farmer upon whom I had been billeted. I had hardly entered the good man's house when he said to me,

"I am very glad to have a Frenchman in the house."

I politely enquired the reason of this preference.

"Well," he said, "you see the barber lives a long way off, so you will be able to shave me."

"But I cannot even shave myself," I replied. "My servant shaves me, and he will shave you also if you like."

"That's very odd," said he. "I was told that all Frenchmen were barbers and fiddlers."

I think I never laughed so heartily. A few minutes later my rations arrived, and my host seeing a large piece of beef amongst them, said,

"You are lucky to be able to come over to America and get some beef to eat."

I assured him that we had beef in France, and excellent beef too.

"That is impossible," he replied, "or you wouldn't be so thin."

Such was,—when Liberty was dawning over the land,—the ignorance shown by the inhabitants of the United States Republic in regard to the French. This lack of knowledge was caused by the difficulty of intercourse with Europe. Their communications were almost entirely cut off, and even Boston and Philadelphia were in the hands of the English; nor were the people on the sea-coast in a more advanced state of civilization than those of the interior. More than a century of progress has been made in less than twenty years. I shall hardly be believed now when I state that, about this time, one of our men having left a pair of jack-boots behind him, the Americans were so astonished at them, that they placed them, as a curiosity, in the New York Museum, where the man who had forgotten them afterwards found them ticketed *French Boots*.

We returned to the camp at Valley Forges about the 15th March. The enemy was still quiet in Philadelphia, dancing and drinking in true English style, and deeming themselves perfectly safe. We were not sufficiently strong to attempt to dislodge them, and were obliged to wait till 15th April, when our recruits and reinforcements were to arrive. We remained inactive till then. The weather was still very cold. A peculiarity of the climate of this country is that often there is no spring, and owing to the absence of one of the most pleasant seasons of the year you pass straight from a long and hard winter to weather of insupportable heat, which has followed, without any intermediate gradations, a severe frost. The autumns, on the other hand, are long and very fine.

By 15th April our reinforcements had arrived, and we were preparing to open the campaign when we learned, with as much surprise as pleasure, that the British army had received orders to evacuate Philadelphia and fall back on New York. Their army was composed of veteran soldiers, was superior to us in numbers, and, moreover, protected by entrenchments. We imagined that the Cabinet at London had probably heard of the expected arrival of the squadron under Comte d'Estaing. But,—whatever was the cause,—the British prepared to leave Philadelphia and retire on New York, which was also in their hands at that time. They had to make a march of thirty leagues, and cross two rivers,—the Delaware at Philadelphia, and North River,—before arriving at New York. We, on our side, prepared to harass their rear-guard.

General Washington—partly out of friendship, and partly from policy—was anxious to afford the

Marquis de la Fayette every opportunity to distinguish himself, and ordered him to take a strong body of troops and cross the Schuylkill, at a spot on the left of the British position, and cut off their rear-guard, if the opportunity should occur. La Fayette had already brilliantly distinguished himself at the Battle of Brandywine, where he had received a ball in the leg.

We left about midnight, silently crossed the Schuylkill, and took up a position in a wood very close to Philadelphia, in order to be able to reconnoitre the enemy at daybreak, and attack if we had the chance. The main body of our army was ready to support us in less than two hours if we signalled for help.

The British, who had spies amongst our men, were soon informed of our plans. The greater part of their army was still in Philadelphia; they made a sortie, carried the weak post we had established on the banks of the Schuylkill to secure our retreat, and then marched in our rear, hoping to catch us between two fires. Our little army, ignorant of the danger of the position, was about to be caught in a trap.

It happened otherwise, however. We had bivouacked and were resting, and waiting for daybreak.

Fortunately ,a surgeon had heard,— I do not know how,— of this night march of the garrison of Philadelphia to cut off our retreat and take us in the rear. In the interests of his own safety, most probably, he had searched along the banks of the river and had found a ford where there was only three or four feet of water. I was lying on the ground, near our general, when the Esculapius came up and whispered the information he had found out, and the discovery of the ford, of which we did not suspect the existence. La Fayette, awakened by the sound of our voices, asked what was the matter, and made the surgeon repeat what he had already told me. Our general was admirably cool, and showed that presence of mind so valuable in a commander in a time of danger. He quietly told the surgeon to return to his post, and as soon as he had left, ordered me to mount my horse, and see for myself if the information was true. I did not go very far before I ascertained that Esculapius was quite correct. I saw the head of a moving column, so I returned at full speed. The next moment the order to march was given, and our retreat was effected quietly and promptly, and our little army crossed the Schuylkill in good order, by the ford which the surgeon had discovered. We were drawn up in order on the right bank, and made the signals previously agreed upon. Our soldiers believed that the march and countermarch formed part of a strategic movement. The enemy did not dare to show himself, being afraid of being caught in a snare.

Our expedition, which had served to puzzle the enemy, and our cleverly executed retreat, brought a good deal of praise to our general, which, to say truth, he deserved, but thanks were also due to the cautious and watchful surgeon who found the ford so opportunely;—nothing was said about *him*, however.

A few days later the British army had completely evacuated Philadelphia. We followed it almost within sight, and at Rareton Rivers, General Lee attacked the enemy's rear-guard, in the morning. This was composed of 7,000 men, the flower of the army, and comprised the regiment of Foot Guards. I was present at this affair, where the Marquis de la Fayette was under Lee's orders. We were thoroughly beaten, our soldiers fled in the greatest disorder, and we could not succeed in rallying them, or even in getting thirty men to keep together. As usually happens, the general who commanded was accused of treason. This was my first battle.

The stragglers re-formed behind our main army, which they met with in their flight, whilst the British, proud of their victory, though it was but a partial one, had the imprudence to pursue us with the reinforcements which they had drawn from the advance guard. General Washington waited for them in a strong position, with all his army drawn up in battle order.

The English had a deep ravine to cross before they could reach us: their brave infantry did not hesitate an instant, but charged us with the bayonet, and was crushed by our artillery. The fine regiment of the guards lost half its men, and its colonel was fatally wounded.

This engagement, called the Battle of Monmouth, from the name of a neighbouring village, began at ten o'clock in the morning: the heat was so excessive that we found soldiers dead without having received a wound. I did not see much of my first battle as we had not remained masters of the field; but that of Monmouth gave me some painful thoughts, even in the midst of the pride and pleasure of victory, and I cannot reproach myself with the callous heartlessness of the man who, on the field of Eylau, amidst the bodies of 24,000 of the victors and vanquished, said, "What a fine slaughter of men!" We slept on the field of battle amongst the dead, whom we had no time to bury. The day had been so hot, in both senses, that everyone had need of rest.

The British army retreated, about midnight, in silence, and we entered the village at six o'clock in the morning. The enemy had left behind some of his baggage and all his wounded; they were to be found in every house, and in the church. Every possible care was taken of them. I cannot even now think without pity of the young officers of the guards who had lost their limbs. Their colonel, one of the handsomest men I have ever seen, and sixty years of age, died of his wounds after suffering for twenty-four hours.

There was no further fighting until the English reached New York. We arrived before the city at almost the same moment as they entered it, and took up our position.

The siege was conducted under circumstances of great difficulty; a British squadron was anchored in the port; the town was protected on one side by North River, and on the other by East River,— both much larger than the Seine, or even the Loire. We should have needed a hundred thousand men if we had wanted to attack the place, and we had but fifteen thousand. The American army remained therefore " in observation," and contented itself with preventing the enemy from foraging in the country round about.

Whilst we were mutually engaged in watching each other, a plot was brewing which, if it had succeeded,—and it was within a hair's breadth of doing so,—would have been disastrous for our army, and perhaps even affected the fate of the newly-born Republic. I allude to General Arnold's conspiracy to betray the Fort of West Point into the hands of the English.

West Point, some twenty leagues from New York on the right bank of North River, was the chief arsenal of the American government. All the heavy artillery was kept there, and also that captured at the surrender of Saratoga. Congress had taken the precaution to make every approach to the place bristle with fortifications. The heights were surmounted by formidable batteries which could bring a heavy cross fire to bear upon several parts of the river, and the passage of the river was also barred—like the port of Constantinople in the time of the Greek Emperors—by a chain, every link of which weighed more than four hundredweight. The fortifications were erected under the direction of MM. Duportail and de Gouvion, officers sent from France.

Amongst the causes which brought about the liberty and independence of the United States, perhaps these impregnable fortifications should count for something.

The British could not hope to capture West Point by main force, for their ships could not approach without running the gauntlet—for fully two miles—of a heavy cross fire from the banks and the neighbouring heights. They resolved to try King Philip's " mule laden with gold." *

The possession of the fort of West Point would allow the enemy to cut off all our communications with the Northern States, from whence we derived all our provisions, particularly cattle. The loss of this place would have been the heaviest possible misfortune for us, and the consequences would have been incalculable. General Arnold commanded the fort.

Major André, a young officer of French extraction,

* Philip of Macedon said, "there was no fortress so impregnable that a mule laden with gold could not enter." The figure is a favourite one with French writers, and has been used by Camille Desmoulins, Châteaubriand, and Heine. ED.

and an adjutant in the British army, often had occasion to visit the American camp to make arrangements concerning the exchange of prisoners. By chance or design, he had made the acquaintance of Arnold. This general, a man of rare courage, had often rendered us signal services, but he had not been rewarded as well as he wished. Major André guessed that he was discontented, and could be easily bought over, and a compact was made between them. Arnold was promised a large sum of money, and a position of equal rank in the British army with full pay. On his side he undertook to surrender the fort. The enemy was to make a night attack by the river, and it was agreed that Arnold was to allow himself to be surprised.

There were still, no doubt, some minor points to be arranged, and it was necessary that the major should meet the general in order to discuss these. André came disguised, and was met by three of our militia men who were patrolling outside our lines, who stopped him and asked the usual questions. The major, who was dressed as a countryman, and badly mounted, replied quietly, and with an affectation of simplicity, that he was a farmer. The three militia men, who by the way were but badly armed, for the musket of one of them had no hammer, were just deciding to let him pass, when he imprudently complained of the delay they had caused him, and was stupid enough to offer them money, and this aroused their suspicions. Thereupon he proposed that they should conduct him to West Point, where he said he wished to go, but one of the militia men remarked that they would have five miles to walk, whereas by going only a mile or so they would meet General Washington, who ought then to be crossing North River on his return from a council of war held at Hartford. This was agreed, and the three militia men conducted their prisoner, without knowing who he was, to Kingsferry, where they awaited at the inn the arrival of the commander-in-chief.

Arnold, however, being suspicious, had had the major followed by a farmer of the district. Being advised by his messenger that André was captured, Arnold at once jumped into a boat manned by English sailors in disguise, and which was waiting for him below the fortifications, and was rowed to the *Vulture*, a British corvette lying about two cannon shot off, and so the unfortunate major was the only victim of Arnold's treason.

All this passed at very little distance from our camp. I had gone, out of curiosity, to see the generals arrive, and so was a witness, by accident, of this great drama. The inn-keeper told me that three militia men had arrested a very suspicious looking person, who had offered them money to let him go free, and showed me the place where this unknown personage was temporarily confined. I went to see him, and spoke to him, but as I did

not know Major André by sight, I imagined the
man to be nothing more than one of the enemy's
spies. I was not the only person astonished a
quarter of an hour later.

General Washington arrived with his staff, and
having been told of the arrest, ordered Colonel Hamilton
to go and examine the accused and bring
back a report. I followed the colonel. The low
room was very dark, and as night was falling, a
light was brought. The colonel sprang back in
astonishment and dismay, on recognizing at the first
glance the unfortunate Major André. The prisoner
wore no military insignia — a regimental jacket under
his countryman's coat, might perhaps have saved
him. Deeply pained by the recognition, Colonel Hamilton
ordered the militia men not to lose sight of
their prisoner for a moment, and hurried back to
the general. "It is Major André," he cried in a
tone of despair. Washington's first words were,
"Take fifty horse, and bring me Arnold dead or
alive." Then he at once gave orders for all the
army to be under arms. His next care was to have
the prisoner searched; there was found on him a
paper containing all the particulars of the plan
agreed upon — the surprise of the fort at West Point,
and a simultaneous attack on our army. God knows
what would have become of the American cause if
the plot had succeeded.

The major was brought into the camp, under a
strong escort, to be tried and sentenced; the least

indulgence shown to him, would, in the circumstances in which we were placed, have been followed by a mutiny in the army.

Few culprits in modern history have inspired and deserved more general interest than this unhappy young man; a distinguished, brave, and active officer, handsome, amiable, and only twenty-six years of age. We received quite a procession of envoys who came to treat for his release. The English generals came in person, and offered almost anything to save his life. There was only one condition we could accept, and that was that Arnold should be delivered into our hands. The English were sorrowfully obliged to refuse this; they could not accede to the terms.

Major André was tried and condemned to be hanged; he did not even obtain the privilege of being shot. I can certify that when they came out after the court-martial the faces of all our generals showed marks of the most profound grief; the Marquis de la Fayette had tears in his eyes. The unfortunate young man met his death courageously; he said loudly that he did not think it dishonourable to have acted as he did against "rebels."

The inevitable doom of Major André only served to accentuate the scorn and hatred that Arnold obtained and deserved. The traitor received his promised reward from the British government, but care was taken not to employ him as a general, the soldiers, both men and officers, being exasperated against him.

His wife and children, whom he had left behind, were in our power. He was base enough to suppose that they would be held responsible for his crime, and insolently wrote to General Washington threatening severe reprisals, and the destruction of Washington's beautiful estate in Virginia if any harm happened to his family. The sole reply Washington made was to order Mrs. Arnold and her children to be conducted into the British lines, with every possible attention. It was, I believe, Colonel Hamilton who was charged with this duty, with instructions to spare them every possible inconvenience.

No event of importance happened during the next few weeks, but we learned that the British government was sending Commissioners to New York to arrange the terms of peace. One of these representatives was Lord Carlisle,* a very young man. He was the cause of a scandal, the odium and ridicule of which affected him alone. He had inserted in the English papers, which were read at New York, a paragraph to the effect that the Marquis de la Fayette had been very well received at the Court of St. James, but a very short time before his departure for America, and therefore it was base ingratitude on his part to play the Don Quixote, and help the colonists in their rebellion

* See Note D.

against their sovereign. The Marquis de la Fayette felt personally insulted by this, and deemed himself justified in demanding satisfaction. A messenger was sent with a flag of truce to carry the challenge, but though the noble lord could not have thought this opponent beneath him in rank, he contented himself with replying that he would leave the quarrel to be settled by Admiral Howe and Comte d'Estaing.* My lord was well known in the fashionable circles of London, and we therefore caused to be inserted in the papers, that he was nothing more than a young dandy, who wore rouge and patches, and was afraid to fight, and the laugh was on our side.

A little later on, Comte d'Estaing appeared before New York with a fleet of twelve vessels of the line and several frigates.

The American army, encouraged by the presence of the French Fleet, advanced the lines close to the city.

D'Estaing had hoped to be able to attack the British fleet in the port, with the advantage of superior force. Admiral Howe's squadron consisted only of seven or eight vessels of 50 guns. The French ships, being much larger, drew too much water, and were afraid of venturing too far in, for fear of running aground. The *Languedoc*, d'Estaing's flag vessel, mounted 110 guns. They were therefore obliged to renounce their original plan, and change their tactics.

* See Note E.

The Marquis de la Fayette gave me a letter of introduction to Comte d'Estaing, which I presented, though I was a trifle nervous at the idea of an interview with such an important personage. He received me very well, and asked a good many questions which I was easily able to answer. I was closeted with him fully two hours. I partook of a most excellent dinner on board the Admiral's vessel, and was therefore much surprised to hear Comte d'Estaing complain that he was in need of many of the necessaries of life;—it certainly did not appear so. I announced the speedy arrival of fifty fat oxen;—which caused such universal pleasure that, before I had finished speaking, the good news was being conveyed by speaking trumpet or signals to all the vessels of the fleet.

All the officers surrounded me, and cross-questioned me closely as to our position, forces, etc. I was quite an important personage. Le Bailly de Suffren *—then only in command of a 50-gun ship—sent for me on board his vessel. I was obliged, in order to please him, to drink such a quantity of punch that when I left the ship I was afraid I should fall into the sea.

I was very happy to meet my cousin, the Chevalier de F——, now the Comte de F——, Grand Cross of the Order of St. Louis, and Vice Admiral: he was then a midshipman on board *La Provence*. He had heard of my escape from Pierre-en-Cize,

* See Note F.

and we now met, eighteen hundred leagues from home, in the midst of a campaign;—the proper place for both of us, however. I was greatly obliged to him for many kindnesses, and more particularly for a small supply of clothes, with which naval officers are always well supplied, and which, as I greatly needed them, I took care not to refuse.

At last I took leave of Comte d'Estaing, who entrusted me with dispatches for the commander-in-chief. I remember that he also gave me some kegs of lemons and pine-apples, which he had found on board a prize he had taken. To regain the camp, I had a voyage of twenty miles to make in a boat. I was so hungry during the night that I devoured several of the pine-apples; and they nearly killed me.

The plan of campaign of 1778 was changed; a combined attack was to be made, the French Fleet was to blockade Newport, Rhode Island, between New York and Boston, whilst a part of the army, under the command of General Sullivan, and comprising the division of the Marquis de la Fayette, was to besiege the place by land.

We effected our landing on this beautiful island in the most orderly manner, and without any difficulties, under the protection of three frigates sent by Comte d'Estaing.

Hardly had the troops disembarked before the militia,—to the number, I believe, of about ten thousand men, horse and foot,—arrived. I have never seen a more laughable spectacle; all the tailors and

apothecaries in the country must have been called
out, I should think;—one could recognize them by
their round wigs. They were mounted on bad nags,
and looked like a flock of ducks in cross-belts.
The infantry was no better than the cavalry, and
appeared to be cut after the same pattern. I guessed
that these warriors were more anxious to eat up
our supplies than to make a close acquaintance
with the enemy, and I was not mistaken,—they
soon disappeared.

A few days after we had disembarked, we opened
our trenches before the place, and the works were
being pushed on with great activity, when the British
fleet appeared before Newport.

Comte d'Estaing at once gave orders to sail; there
was little wind, but what there was was favourable.
Our fleet defiled majestically in front of the enemy's
earthworks; each vessel as she passed gave a broad-
side of half her guns, amongst them many 24- and
36-pounders, to which the forts replied with their
10- and 12-pounders. Our fleet gave chase to the
British, who made all sail. Both fleets were soon
lost to sight. We awaited the news of a victory,
but our fleet was dispersed by a terrible storm, and
the admiral's vessel, the *Languedoc*, dismasted by
the gale, was very nearly captured by the enemy.
The *César*, a vessel of 74 guns, commanded by
M. de Raimondis, separated from the rest of the
squadron, had a very severe engagement with some
of the enemy's vessels. The captain lost his right

arm, but managed to save his ship, which we thought had been captured. It was in the midst of this tempest that Admiral Byron's fleet arrived and joined that of Admiral Howe. The enemy then had the advantage in strength.

The siege still went on, but when M. d'Estaing re-appeared before Newport he told us he must withdraw the three frigates he had left to protect us, and we must raise the siege. D'Estaing took all the fleet to Boston for repairs.

General Sullivan, angry at finding himself no longer supported by the French fleet, went so far as to insult our nation, and call the French traitors. Our two generals were almost on the point of fighting a duel. The Marquis de la Fayette complained bitterly, and with good reason, to Washington, of the treatment he had received. The retreat was made in good order, and we rejoined the main army.

In this expedition the commanders, both by land and sea, were dissatisfied with each other and themselves, but for me the siege had been rather pleasant, and on one occasion I received compliments which were as numerous as they were sincere. The occasion was as follows:

The Chevalier de Preville, who commanded the three frigates intended to protect our communications, wrote to me to ask if he could obtain some supplies for his sailors. I handed his letter to the Marquis de la Fayette, and General Sullivan authorized me to take a detachment and forage between the two camps.

For twenty-four hours I was in chief command, and had to make all the military and gastronomic dispositions required. The space between the enemy's forts and our lines was covered with houses and gardens, the owners of which had deserted them, not caring about living between two fires. My work had to be carried out right under the enemy's nose, and I fully expected there would be some bullets to receive. I had requisitioned all the carts I could find, and filled them with fruit and,—so well does heaven protect good works,—not a shot was fired at us.

The frigates, being informed by signal, of the success of my expedition, sent off a number of boats, and I protected the convoy down to the beach. You should have seen with what gusto the sailors devoured the apples, and with what alacrity they unloaded the carts of potatoes, carrots, and other vegetables. Their gratitude was all the greater as they had been some time without any fresh vegetables. They hailed me as the good fairy of the fleet, and when I went on board I was enthusiastically welcomed.

The French government at last decided to recognize the United States as independent, and sent out M. Gerard as French Ambassador to Congress. It was quite time France took a step of this kind, for the help that she had sent through Caron de Beaumarchais had not given much satisfaction. The letters that he wrote to Congress, for instance, displayed a levity which amounted almost to insolence. I have kept a copy of one of his letters.

"GENTLEMEN,

"I beg to inform you that the ship *Amphitrite*, of 400 tons burden, will leave with the first fair wind for whatever port of the United States she may be able to reach. The cargo of the vessel, which is consigned to you, consists of 4,000 muskets, 80 barrels of gunpowder, 8,000 pairs of boots, 3,000 woollen blankets, also some engineer and artillery officers; *item*, a German Baron, formerly aide-de-camp to Prince Henry of Prussia, of whom you can make a general.

"I am, Gentlemen,

"Your obedient Servant,

"C. DE BEAUMARCHAIS." *

The members of Congress were very indignant about this letter, with the contents of which they made all us Frenchmen acquainted, but it was on a par with all that he did, and what might have been expected from such a man.

The German Baron of whom he spoke so slightingly, was Baron Steuben, a great tactician, who was accompanied also by the Chevalier de Ternan, a very distinguished officer. I have already named M. Duportail, M. Duplessis-Mauduit, and M. de la Rouarie. When the last-named presented himself before Congress, he was attended by his valet, a tall, handsome, and very brave man, named Lefevre.

* See Note G.

M. de la Rouarie at once received his commission as colonel, and, so simple and inexperienced were the members of the Committee, that they offered a similar commission to the valet on the strength of his good looks. He thanked Congress for the proffered honour, but begged leave to refuse it. Congress then consisted of thirteen members, one from each State of the Union, but men very different from us in their habits and ways. They took their seats in the Congress Hall, as we should enter a reading room in Paris, and the wisdom of their magnanimous resolutions was even surpassed by the simplicity of their manners.

After the siege of Newport was raised, we returned to the camp. General Washington and Congress decided to sent La Fayette to France to ask for further supplies of men and money, the American paper money having fallen into utter discredit.

Great haste was made to finish building the frigate *Alliance*, which was to be a fast sailer, armed with thirty-six 12-pounders. The command of the new vessel was given to a Frenchman, Captain Landais of St. Malo, but the ship was under the orders of M. de la Fayette, and the captain was to land him wherever he wished. To complete the crew we, unfortunately, took seventy English prisoners. They were excellent sailors, and as they had all taken an oath of fidelity, it was thought they could be trusted.

The winter was very severe, and the ship was

not fitted out till the end of January. The port of Boston was then frozen, and we were obliged to cut a passage for the ship through the ice. The wind was extremely violent, though favourable. We put up our mainsail only and that alone took us along at the rate of ten knots an hour. There were many French officers on board, amongst others M. de Raimondis, the captain of the *César*, who had lost his right arm in the last naval battle.

Off the Bank of Newfoundland we were assailed by a terrible tempest. It lasted so long, and grew so much worse, that first inquietude, then alarm, and at last consternation, seized everybody on board.

M. de la Fayette was invariably very ill at sea: he was down on the sick list. He often sent me to enquire after old Captain Raimondis, who suffered much pain from his amputation,—sufferings which were increased by the heavy rolling of the ship. The old sailor did not take a hopeful view of the situation; he told me that he had never, in all his voyages, met with such a fearful tempest. I carried these remarks back to M. de la Fayette, but to comfort him as well as myself, I told him that I thought the state of health of Captain Raimondis must necessarily influence his mind, and make matters look worse than they really were. M. de la Fayette lay on his back and soliloquized on the emptiness of glory and fame.

"Diable!" he said, philosophically, "I have done well certainly. At my time of life—barely twenty years of age—with my name, rank, and fortune, and after having married Mlle de Noailles, to leave everything and serve as a breakfast for codfish!"

For my own part I was better off; I had nothing to lose and no one to regret me. I went back to the old sailor. He occupied a cabin on the deck below that where M. de la Fayette was lodged, so that in going from one to the other I met with frequent falls, and had plenty of bruises to show as the result of my messages. It was impossible to keep one's feet, owing to the continual heavy seas which struck the ship. There was some talk of cutting the masts. One of my comrades M. de N——, became so excited that I saw him charge his pistols, so as to shoot himself rather than be drowned. There did not seem to me a pin to choose between either fate, but his last hour had not yet come. This unlucky fellow had a mania for suicide. In 1792, after the 10th August, he was an officer in the Constitutional Guards, and when the "patriots" came to drag him away to the Abbaye, he escaped from their hands by passing his sword through his body. At the end of three days,—which seemed very long, I must admit,—the tempest ceased, and during the rest of the voyage we had favourable weather.

But heaven had yet another trial in store for us. Whilst we were at dinner one day, thinking no more of bad weather, but of France, from which we were now only some five hundred miles distant, one of the crew entered, and asked to speak to

M. de la Fayette. He took the Marquis on one side, and told him a good deal in a very few words; namely, that the English sailors had laid a plot to kill us, take possession of the vessel, and turn her head towards England. This was to be effected at five o'clock in the evening, when the English sailors came off their watch. Our informant added, that many of the men, especially the ringleaders, would be found to have arms concealed in their hammocks. He had only joined in the plot, he said, in order to be able to save us.

There was not a moment to be lost. We numbered in all fourteen officers. We began by securing the man who had warned us, and Duplessis-Mauduit stood over him with a cocked pistol in his hand. Some of us then went to fetch the bravest and trustiest of our sailors, who came quickly and ready armed. Thirty of us went down between decks, and, as the hammock of each of the ringleaders was pointed out to us by the man who had betrayed the conspiracy, the cords were cut with one blow of a hatchet, and the man thrown out, seized, and bound, before he was half awake. The scoundrels were so taken by surprise that they made no resistance. At first they all denied the existence of a plot, but on being questioned separately, the fear of being hanged on the spot made them confess their crime, one of the motives for which, it appeared, was that they had noticed amongst the baggage of M. de la Fayette, some very heavy cases which they supposed contained treasure. The informer was, of course, rewarded as he deserved. None of us went to bed that night; we had to watch over sixty men, bound, and shut up between decks. In the cabin which served as our council-chamber, nothing was to be seen but loaded pistols and drawn swords.

At daybreak we found that a Swedish merchant vessel was close to us. Captain Landais made the master come on board. The poor man's terror at seeing our cabin was ludicrous, the sight of all these deadly weapons made him imagine that his last hour had come. We tried to re-assure him by signs, for he did not know a word of French. For two whole days he was too frightened to either eat or drink, but he ended by finding our dinners very good, and our wine excellent. Captain Landais maintained that the Swede was a legitimate capture, but, when we arrived in France, we were forced to let him go.

We were all anxious to see land, for we were tired out, and we were worried moreover, by the fear of meeting a hostile vessel stronger than ourselves, in which case it was tolerably certain that the men we were guarding below decks would have helped her. We had lost our top masts in the tempest, so flight would have been impossible. We were not yet in sight of land,—though it could have been at no great distance,—when an English cruiser of 16 guns, saw us and gave chase. As we showed no guns she no doubt thought ours was a vessel of the French East India Company, and a rich prize. So sure of this were her crew, that, as she neared us they mounted the rigging and cheered. When she was within half range she fired a shot to make us show our colours. We instantly ran up the American flag, and followed that by giving her a broad side.

She quickly saw her mistake, and lowered her flag. We contented ourselves with sending a boat's crew on board, and throwing all her guns and powder into the sea. We took a lot of Madeira wine, which we found on board, and then let her go in this pitiable condition. In our peculiar situation that was the most we could do.

When we came within sight of the French coast, I noticed that our captain was making towards the English Channel. He would no doubt have been glad to revisit St. Malo, his native town. I told M. de la Fayette, who caused him to put the vessel about and make for Brest, where we disembarked.

CHAPTER IV.

I visit my father, and am restored to his good graces— Arrival in Paris—Welcomed by all my relatives—Unexpected appointment as deputy-captain—Ordered to Lorient—Paul Jones and Captain Landais—Counter orders—Re-embark on frigate "Alliance" to rejoin Washington's army.—In the absence of Paul Jones, the command of the frigate is given to Landais—He becomes insane during the voyage—Removed from his command by order of the passengers—The campaign of 1781—Siege of York Town— The Capitulation of Cornwallis—End of the American War on the Continent—I return to France on the "Ariel," commanded by Chevalier de Capellis—We fight and capture the British vessel "Dublin"—We enter Corunna in triumph—Fêtes, Balls, etc.—A religious difficulty—We narrowly escape figuring in an auto-da-fé—The "Ariel" weighs anchor—Arrival at Lorient.

OUR first care was to conduct to the town jail the rascally British sailors we had had so much trouble to guard. Instructions were given that they should be taken back to America, at the first opportunity, and there judged according to the laws of the country.

The naval officers received us well, but we could not make a long stay at Brest. Everyone of us wished to turn his steps towards home. The Marquis de la Fayette, who no longer philosophized now that he was safe on dry land, went to the Hôtel de Noailles. His arrival was the news of the day, both at Paris and Versailles. The Queen of France did him the honour to bring Madame de la Fayette in her own carriage. She was surprised to meet her husband, for she had not been apprised of his return.

As for me, I took the *diligence* and made my way first to Clermont, and then to the paternal mansion, the Château of Pontgibaud. Gratitude took precedence of natural affection, however, for as the places happened to be on my road, I first went to Nantes, and thanked M. de la Ville-Hélis, and then to La Rochelle to thank M. Seigneur for past services. I did not want to surprise my father by arriving unexpectedly, and therefore took care to write and announce my return. Along with my own very respectful letter, I enclosed one which the Marquis de la Fayette had been kind enough to write to my father.

In spite of these precautions, I felt a sort of fear as I entered his room, and appeared before him for the first time. We were both equally embarrassed. His clouded brow betokened a storm, not an approaching storm, however, but one that is dying away in the distance. He addressed some reproaches to me, but they were merely a matter of form, intended to keep up the appearance of paternal dignity, and mainly concerned the heavy expenses which my journey from Paris to Pierre-en-Cize, and my imprisonment there had cost him.

I very naturally observed that perhaps if he had given me all that money he would have made a better use of it, and so should I. This very sensible reflection was too much for his gravity; he quite unbent, and it was with difficulty that he could prevent himself from laughing.

At the end of two hours he was no longer the same man, his curiosity had got the better of him, and he wanted me to give a full account of my Odyssey, my escape, voyage across the Atlantic, shipwreck, campaigns, and all. He made me read to him many times M. de la Fayette's letter, which corroborated all my statements. I say advisedly that he made me read it to him, for he had lost one of his eyes, many years before, at the Battle of Dettingen, and old age had enfeebled the sight of the other. I passed a fortnight at home, and by that time every cloud had passed away, and the sky was blue. I was so well restored to my father's affection that when I was leaving him to return to Paris to ask for a position in the army, he made me a present of 200 louis, increased my allowance to 1000 crowns, and gave me the address of a banker whom he had instructed to repay M. de la Fayette all the advances he had made on my account. He even offered to purchase a cavalry company for me if I could obtain one. He gave me besides a letter of thanks to my general. It was with a heart full of gratitude that I left him and started for Paris.

The nine beatitudes awaited me there. Certainly there must be some communication between heaven and earth, for no sooner was I restored to my respected father's good graces than all sorts of good fortune fell upon me.

At Paris I lodged in furnished apartments, not having the least idea where I should find any of my numerous relations, whom I believed to all be at their country houses at that season of the year. My uncle, the President de Salaberry took me to his house, and asked me to consider it as my home. He was a kind, good man, but that did not prevent him from being murdered during the Revolution— perhaps caused his death even. He heaped kindnesses upon me with the same serenity of conscience with which, as my father's brother-in-law he had loaded me with abuse in my earlier days; but at that time he had been prejudiced against me by falsehoods and innuendoes which he was now annoyed with himself for believing.

When he had finished welcoming and embracing me, my kind but over-hasty uncle handed me a letter from my father, dated at Pontgibaud, 19th April, 1779. I shall never forget the date—*albo dies notanda lapillo*. I pressed to my heart this letter, which was addressed to my uncle, and in which I was happy to read these words, which shewed me that my father's present kindness was due to his sense of justice.

"Monsieur le Comte," wrote the secretary, for the good old man was obliged to dictate his letters, "desires that the Chevalier shall want for nothing; his intention being to compensate him amply for the misfortunes he has suffered by the injustice which was done him. He has been the victim of a sordid conspiracy which was discovered too late."

I thought no more of the injury that had been done me, except as a pleasing reminiscence, and dated my happiness back to the day of my escape, which after all had been something of a feat.

But I was far from knowing all the favours that fortune had in store for me. After I had been three weeks in Paris, the Marquis de la Fayette informed me that the King had given him a regiment of dragoons, and that His Majesty had granted me a commission as *capitaine de remplacement*, which entitled me to half-pay. The Minister of War confirmed the good news in an official letter, in which he said that by the wish of an important personage who did not wish his name to be known,—though I easily guessed it,—and who had taken me under his protection, the price of the brevet, that is to say 7000 francs, was remitted, and I had nothing to pay for my commission. I had no further happiness to desire, for, since the end of the "Seven Years' War", France had been at peace, and the army swarmed with young officers with aristocratic names.

It was more difficult to be a cavalry captain in 1779 than it was to be a colonel twenty or thirty years later.

The French Government was then meditating a descent on England. A large army assembled in Brittany and Normandy, under the command of the Comte de Vaux.

Many transport ships were also collected at Havre and St. Malo. M. de la Fayette sent for me and told me that I was to start for Lorient, in company with the Chevalier de Gimat,—who had been one of his *aides-de-camp* in the American War,—and there wait for orders. There were some hints of a secret expedition. My heart beat with joy. My comrade, who was much older than I, a colonel, and a very experienced officer, was in the secret, but it was in vain that I tried to draw it out of him. He confined himself to repeating that I was very lucky, and that I should find that the patronage of the Marquis de la Fayette would be of great service to me. Beyond this he would tell me nothing.

Many armed vessels were awaiting us in the port of Lorient; the *Bon Homme Richard*, a vessel belonging to the India Company mounting 54 guns of various calibres; the frigate *Alliance*, on which we had made the voyage back to France; the *Pallas*, 32 guns, commanded by Captain Cottineau of Nantes, an able officer of the merchant service, etc. These were under the orders of the celebrated American commodore, Paul Jones, who commanded the *Bon Homme Richard.* A number of brigs and corvettes completed the little squadron.

We were to receive, on board these vessels and some transport ships, about 3000 men drafted from different regiments of the French army, and under the command of Marquis de la Fayette. I know now, what I did not know at that time, though I much wished to, that the object of this expedition was to make a descent upon Ireland, whilst the army of Comte de Vaux, protected by the combined fleets of France and Spain, under Comte d'Orvilliers, were to co-operate at the same time in a similar descent on the English coast. For some reason, unknown to me, the execution of this plan was deferred, and finally abandoned by the French Government.

During the six weeks that I spent in idleness at Lorient, I was eye-witness of a most curious, ridiculous, and incredible incident. A man in uniform dashed up the staircase, rushed into the room where I was sitting, and begged me to protect him. He looked scared, and anxious. It was no other than our brave,—indeed more than brave,—Commodore, the famous Paul Jones.

"Shut the door," he cried. "That scoundrel Captain Landais met me in the town and wants to fight me. He is pursuing me from street to street, sword in hand. I do not know how to fence and I do not want to be killed by that rascal."

I closed the door and double-locked it, but the

Captain never came. Certainly Paul Jones acted very sensibly, for the match was not equal; Captain Landais with his drawn sword would have made short work of him, and Paul Jones had nothing but blows to gain by the encounter. This adventure does not in the least detract from his reputation. His recent fight with the *Serapis*, that he captured by boarding, placed his courage above all suspicion, and put him on an equality with all the boldest, luckiest, and bravest sailors of ancient or modern times.

His quarrel with Captain Landais, of which this fight was a part, was not for the possession of a Helen, but for the command of the frigate *Alliance*, which had been ordered to sail at once for America, for, owing to some veering of the political compass, everything had been changed.

Six thousand Frenchmen, under the command of Comte de Rochambeau, and including a great number of young noblemen of the Court, anxious to have the privilege of serving as volunteers, were sent to the aid of the Americans, and embarked on a fleet of vessels, commanded by the Chevalier de Ternan, which was to sail from Brest. M. de la Fayette having sent in his resignation as Colonel of Dragoons, had taken leave of the King in the uniform of a Major General of the United States' army, and was already on board the French frigate *Aigle*, commanded by M. de la Touche Treville. La Fayette was to take the command of a division of Washington's army which was then encamped in Jersey Province, near New York. We received orders to join him, and embarked on the frigate *Alliance*, which was to sail without delay. Captain Landais had secured the command without striking a blow.

The conqueror of the *Serapis* had hardly left my sheltering roof than he went to Paris to show himself. The Parisians went to their windows to see him pass, and thronged to the Opera the night he went there. Marshal de Biron, who did the honours of the capital to all the great personages, received Paul Jones with every mark of respect, and placed the regiment of Gardes Françaises under arms, in order to show it to the commander of the *Bon Homme Richard*. But during this time, Captain Landais remained at Lorient, and the American Minister we were to take back, being in haste to depart, took it upon himself not to wait for Paul Jones, and nominated Landais to the command.

We had sailed about a week when Paul Jones returned from Paris, and found himself without a command. We had on board two commissioners from Congress, and we were bound for Boston. It was decreed, apparently, that I should meet with strange adventures during my transatlantic voyages. On this voyage the captain went out of his mind. We had previously noticed some peculiarities in his manner, and we were soon to acquire the certainty that he was insane.

His madness broke out one day at dinner, the cause being a turkey that he was carving. Mr. Lee, one of the commissioners, who sat beside him, took the liver, and was about to eat it when Landais rose in a fury, and threatened to kill him with the carving-knife. Everyone rose, and the two nephews of the American commissioner ran to call some of the crew to prevent their uncle being murdered. Landais shouted out that the best morsel belonged by right to the captain. He said and did all sorts of foolish things. I took up my dinner knife in order to defend myself, for he seemed as though he were coming at me to take vengeance on me because I was roaring with laughter. He was raving mad. A number of the sailors ran up, and the commissioners ordered them to seize and bind the captain, which was done. We drew up an official report of the incident; and the command of the vessel was given to the first officer.

Under the direction of the new captain, we made a good passage, and disembarked at the end of ten or twelve days. Our course of action (in deposing the captain) was approved by the authorities at Boston. Such was the end of Captain Landais, the rival of Paul Jones—as far as my knowledge of him is concerned, at all events, for I never heard what became of him afterwards.

I hastened to rejoin the American army, which three weeks after my arrival, marched for Virginia.

This was in 1780. The little army of Comte de

Rochambeau was blockaded in Rhode Island, where it had disembarked about the middle of the year. It was powerless to undertake any decisive action until the arrival of the French fleet.

It was not till 1781, almost a year after the landing, that the fleet under Comte de Grasse* entered Chesapeake Bay. During this long interval, the American army, to which I belonged, performed no action of historical interest. I, for my part, shared with the others the dangers, and took part in the few indecisive skirmishes of the campaign, which we passed in marching and counter-marching, with occasional out-post affairs—in fact it was a war of observation.

The approach of the French fleet favoured a plan of attack which might result in a general and decisive engagement, and Comte de Rochambeau at last left Rhode Island. Washington's army embarked, joined the French forces, and we hemmed in the principal British army which then occupied Virginia and was in position at York Town. Lord Cornwallis, the commander-in-chief, was attacked by us on 6th October. One of the two principal redouts was carried by the Marquis de la Fayette and the Americans a quarter of an hour before the French, headed by the regiment of "Grenadiers de Deux-Ponts" captured the other. The French and Americans emulated each other in courage and obstinacy, and the English also fought like devils. But British pride was humbled

* See Note H.

and Marquis Cornwallis was obliged to capitulate.

The young Duc de Lauzun * was sent by the two generals to arrange the terms of surrender. He went alone, waving his white handkerchief in his hand, for the chivalric Duc de Lauzun never acted like anyone else would in the same circumstances. The British army did not come out with drums beating, colours flying, and all the honours of war, but was forced to defile between a double row of French and Americans, and lay down their arms, to the shame and confusion of their brave and unfortunate soldiers. Marquis Cornwallis wished to give up his sword to Comte de Rochambeau, but the French general made a sign with his hand to show that the honour of receiving it belonged to Washington as the commander-in-chief.

The English, now shut in New York State, were no longer in a condition to continue the campaign, and there followed a kind of tacitly arranged truce extending over the eighteen months which preceded the declaration of peace. The combined armies of Washington and Comte de Rochambeau were compelled to remain inactive, for the surrender at York Town had settled the question of American Independence, though the French and English continued to fight at sea for a few months longer. Being unacquainted with that kind of diplomacy which leads to nothing more than an exchange of cannon shot between hostile fleets, and finding that not

* See Note I.

another musket was to be fired in war on the American continent, M. de la Fayette left for France, and I did the same, for we had nothing in common with the little French army which remained in the United States until further orders.

Comte de Rochambeau's officers had nothing better to do, I suppose, than travel about the country. When we think of the false ideas of government and philanthropy which these youths acquired in America, and propagated in France with so much enthusiasm and such deplorable success,—for this mania of imitation powerfully aided the Revolution, though it was not the sole cause of it,—we are bound to confess that it would have been better, both for themselves and us, if these young philosophers in red-heeled shoes had stayed at the Court.

But a truce to these reflections which have nothing to do with my memoirs. In the autumn of 1781, my friend, the Chevalier de Capellis, was about to sail for France in the frigate *Ariel*, which he commanded, and he took me on board. The *Ariel* was a prize captured by Comte d'Estaing's squadron; she was a very fast sailer, but only carried eighteen 9-pounders.

We started with a favourable wind, but a few days later were assailed by a tempest, which are frequent in these seas. My friend swore, as all sailors do, that this should be his last voyage; he was rich and would certainly never expose himself again to any of the dangers of this cursed profession. I did not believe a word of it, and I was quite right. He related to me the history of his brother, who had perished at sea,—this story always occurred to his recollection whenever the weather was bad. The storm, however, was not to be compared to that which I had encountered on my first return, when on the frigate *Alliance*.

After a voyage of fifty-five days, we sighted the coasts of Spain. I must not omit to mention that when fifty leagues from land we had the pleasure of meeting the *Dublin*, armed with twelve 9-pounders. She rightly guessed that our vessel was of English build, and supposed that we were English, but she very soon found out her mistake, greatly to our satisfaction, though not to hers. Both ships having shown their flags, a cannonade ensued, which lasted three quarters of an hour, at the end of which time the *Dublin* struck, for we were twice her size. She was loaded with merchandise.

The vessel and cargo belonged to the *Ariel*. I could not help laughing at my friend Capellis. During the fight he was everywhere at once, animating the gunners, swearing, and crying that our fire was not fast enough or heavy enough. When the *Dublin* struck, our gunners between decks, being unable to see on account of the smoke, or to hear on account of the noise, still went on firing. Capellis then felt that the enemy's vessel was his property, and that every extra bit of damage done her was a loss to him. He quite changed his tone and cried, "Cease firing! cease firing," but no one heard him. "Upon my word, that fellow has fired again!" he shouted as he saw one of the gunners let fly another shot. His anger was really comic, and I believe he would have killed the man if he had not been restrained.

We entered the port of Corunna in triumph, with our prize, and moored close to the *Argonaut*, a French vessel of 74 guns, commanded by M. de Caqueray. He was about to give a fête on board that day, and we received invitations.

Even before we touched land, I thus enjoyed the honour and pleasure of seeing the ladies of Corunna, who had been invited, so to speak, on purpose to meet us, but before the ball we were regaled with an unexpected sight which much astonished as.

Before we had even cast our anchor, we were surrounded by a host of small boats containing women bringing fruit, and who climbed up the ship's sides as though they had been sailor boys. Many of the women were young and pretty, and did not sell fruit. In spite of orders they stormed our vessel, and, as the sailors favoured them, they were soon all over the ship,—except in the gunroom there were women everywhere; we could not help laughing at this strange invasion.

The fête given by M. de Caqueray was a very grand one, and the ladies appeared to me charming, for it was so long since I had seen any.

I was not quite so enthusiastic about the city of Corunna which these beautiful ladies and damsels inhabited. I had just left the United States, a new country where the towns were all new and where the greatest cleanliness prevailed even in the most humble habitation; where nothing to excite disgust was ever seen, and there were no rags, and no beggars. At Corunna, I found old houses, mendicity at every corner, an atmosphere infected with smoke, and the smell of fried oil, and in fact all the innate dirtiness of people whose natural element is filth. Add to this the clatter of carts with wooden wheels, rumbling over the most uneven pavement in the world. Jean Jacques would have quitted Corunna an hour after he entered it, for he pretends that he was obliged to leave his lodgings in Paris simply because he heard a water carrier cry *A l'eau!* in an unmusical voice.

As I had come from America, you may imagine that I was asked thousands of questions. The Duke of Medina-Celi, the colonel of a regiment then quartered in Corunna, asked as many questions as the Bailli in the *Ingénu*,* but otherwise he was a very agreeable young man. Spaniards and French were then good friends, for the two nations had allied their forces against England, and both armies wore a cockade in which the French white was mingled with the Spanish red and black.

We were detained by contrary winds, and we

* One of Voltaire's short stories.

profited by this accident to visit the port and arsenal of Ferrol.

We were told that it was "a miniature Brest." I noted that, like our great marine arsenal, it was entered by a narrow strait, but I do not otherwise intend to compare the two. All that I will say is, that I have seen Brest and I have seen Ferrol.

On our return to Corunna we were invited to a ball given specially in our honour. Madame Tenoria, the wife of the naval commissioner, held a faro bank at her house every night. I remember that I once had a mind to play there, and I lost a hundred louis,—one of the clearest of all my recollections of my wanderings.

I saw my pieces of gold disappear without ever uttering an impatient word,—but the devil lost nothing by my silence. Inwardly I was harrowed with grief and rage. My face looked calm, but nevertheless I was just on the point of kicking over the cursed gaming-table, when I was restrained by a remark of one of the bystanders. I distinctly heard someone near me say, "What a fine gambler that young officer is; he loses and never says a word." I felt that I was something of a hero, and that as a soldier I had to sustain the honour of the cloth. I put my hand back on the table, but if anyone could have looked under my coat they would have seen that I had buried the nails of the other hand in my flesh. Nevertheless I left behind me at Corunna, not only all my money, but the reputation of being a first-rate gambler. The experience served me in good stead, however, for since then I have never played again.

An incident of another nature happened to us whilst we were at Corunna,—one that might have had serious consequences for us, though we were not to blame.

We passed our evenings in one or other of the best houses of the city, returning on board about ten o'clock, at which time the boat was waiting for us. One night, when the weather was very bad, we happened to meet a religious procession in a narrow street; the *viaticum* was being carried to some great personage, I should imagine by the number of people who followed the dais; there were a great many women in the crowd. We three officers stood on one side respectfully, removed our hats, and as it was pouring with rain, we received all the water from the gutters on our unprotected heads, and were drenched to the skin. When the procession had passed, and was about thirty yards away, we thought we could with decency put on our hats, but the people tore them off again, crying and shouting something we could not understand, as we did not know Spanish. With that we all three drew our swords, whereupon these exceedingly pious Christians all tumbled over one another to get out of the way, and left us a clear road. We hastened our steps and took the first cross street we could find. The people, not wishing to lose anything of the ceremony, did not pursue us. Not knowing the town well, we probably did not take the shortest road to the boat, but we found it at last, and were very glad to take our seats in it.

I mentally recounted to myself all that had happened to me since Pierre-en-Cize, and I could not prevent saying to myself, all that is needed is to see myself flogged to slow music through this cursed town, and then figure in an *auto-da-fé* with a *benito* on my head. But that would have been too much spite on the part of fortune, to heap so many misfortunes upon a simple individual like me. Providence watched over us. Our adventure had, however, created some excitement in the town, and the commandant requested us to give him the true account of the matter. When he had heard it, he recommended us not to set foot on shore for some days, and he promised to come and dine on board with us the following day. He was an Irishman, very kind and very witty, and we agreed together perfectly, but we were disenchanted with Corunna, and a few days later, the wind being favourable, we weighed anchor, and, after a good passage of a few days, landed at Lorient.

CHAPTER V.

Proposed expedition to Senegal—A visit to Pierre-en-Cize—The reception I met with there—The reputation I had left behind me—Institution of the Order of Cincinnatus, which I am one of the first to receive—The pleasures of peace; mathematics and the violin—Expedition to Cochin-China—An Oriental Young Pretender—Eastern presents—The year 1789—Physical and political signs of an approaching Revolution—Infatuation of the people at Versailles and Paris—Delille—Nostradamus—Cazotte—La Fayette and my French comrades of the Order of Cincinnatus side with the Revolutionary party—I emigrate with my brother—The campaign in Champagne—The retreat—We arrive in Switzerland and establish ourselves at Lausanne—An account of the members of our little family—How an important house of business was founded—Unexpected news—I am called to the United States to receive ten thousand dollars, back pay and interest—I embark at Hamburg and go to receive my money.

I, AND my friend the Chevalier de Capellis at once started for Paris.

We went together to Versailles to see Marshal de Castries, who was then Minister of the Navy; he cross-questioned me closely upon the glorious battle of York Town, an event which has become

famous. I noticed that, as we were retiring, the
Minister took my friend Capellis on one side, and I
heard the marshal tell him, for I listened, to come
on a certain day at a certain hour, when he would
hear some news that would please him. I was not
interested, for the affair seemed no business of mine,
but two days later, Capellis came and told me that
the marshal intended to send a small expedition to
seize the English factories at Senegal, which, he
heard, were but poorly defended, and could easily
be taken by 150 men: Capellis was appointed to
the chief command of the expedition, which was to
consist of a frigate and a corvette. He had asked
and obtained for me the command of the small body
of soldiers which was to take part in this bold
adventure.

The expectation of figuring as a conqueror greatly
delighted me. It was not much of an affair, I
confess, but everything must have a beginning.
The expedition occupied all my thoughts. I already
pictured to myself the Marabouts, the local clergy,
paying their homage to the conquerors; I shook
hands with the King of Dahomey, and replaced
Robert D—— in the affections of the little Queen
of Cayor—to say nothing of the elephants' teeth and
gold which I was sure to find in the English
factories when I had taken them.

Whilst I was building these fine castles in the
air I wrote off to my father, not doubting for an
instant but that he would share the pleasure I felt

at the prospect. I told him I was the happiest man alive, for that I was about to proceed shortly on an expedition in which I should have an opportunity of distinguishing myself and gaining both " glory and profit." My father,—an old man with very positive ideas on certain subjects, and high-minded and chivalric,—was not impressed by the two words " glory" and " profit." He looked at the matter in a different light, and,—to my great surprise, I confess,—wrote me, by return of post, a short, sharp note, in which he said that as soon as he had finished reading my letter he had put it in the fire, in order to destroy all record of sentiments which did me but little honour. The words " glory " and " profit", he added, should never come together, either in the mouth or under the pen of a French officer, and he begged that I would never write him anything of the same kind again. This paternal rebuke, which was not undeserved, was all that I ever got out of the proposed expedition, which came to nothing.

As I had leave of absence, and was not obliged to rejoin my regiment then in garrison at Auch, I went to Auvergne and visited my father, who, now that he had given me a bit of his mind, was no longer angry with me. Finding myself, after an interval of three years, within a hundred miles of my former political residence, the castle of Pierre-en-Cize, of which I was no longer in fear, I one day proposed to our worthy neighbour M. d'Al——, whose friendship had been so useful to me, that we should take a ride over to Lyon. I wanted him to see with his own eyes the scene of the events I had narrated to him, that he might not believe my account on hearsay only.

We arrived at Lyon. It is customary on visiting the castle to give at the gate your name and that of the hotel at which you are staying. The corporal who came out to question us, looked at me, and recognized me, although I was enveloped in the long cloak of the dragoon uniform.

"Oh, sir," he said laughingly, "there is no need to ask your name; we are not likely to forget it."

The corporal had belonged to the guard on the day when I had my fight with it. He eagerly asked us where we were lodging, and an hour after our arrival we received from M. de Bellecize, the governor of the castle, a pressing invitation to dine with him on the following day.

We accepted, and were warmly welcomed. It was not surprising that in the short interval of three years few changes should have taken place in a stationary garrison like that of Pierre-en-Cize, and that there should still be many amongst them who, like the worthy corporal, had seen me and known me. During dessert, a deputation came from the soldiers to welcome me, and to recite some verses, whichthey had made up amongst themselves, in my honour. The intention was good, and I took it as such and duly rewarded it, and the honest fellows were as pleased with my gold as I was with their verses.

After dinner, M. de Bellecize ordered the gaoler to show us the room I had occupied, but strictly advised him not to allow a prisoner named De Livry to see me. My name was never out of the head of this unfortunate young man. He was always talking about my exploit, and had made several attempts to escape, and complained bitterly to heaven that one man should always fail where another had succeeded. The governor thought it likely that the prisoner might go out of his mind if he saw the person about whom he talked so much, so we did not meet.

On 20th January, 1783, England, by a solemn treaty of peace, recognized, in clear and precise terms, the Independence of the United States.

One of the first acts of the young Republic was to found the Order of Cincinnatus, and make it hereditary. It had a sky blue watered ribbon with a white border, below which was an eagle with outstretched wings in enamelled gold. We, in France, did not know what was going on beyond the seas, when suddenly the Marquis de la Fayette was surprised to receive a packet of a dozen eagles to be distributed between him and his companions in arms. I was one of the twelve honoured by this mark of distinction. I have heard that Comte de Rochambeau received thirty-six eagles of Cincinnatus for himself and the principal officers of his forces.

Claims and pretended claims to this honour came

from all quarters, indeed there has been quite a mania, in France, for orders, ever since the days of Louis XIV. The French navy also asked, and with just cause, for some of these orders, and I would not swear that, within a year, Beaumarchais himself had not received it;—the slightest connection with America was considered sufficient basis for a claim to this honour. I felt great pleasure in being one of the first to receive the Order of Cincinnatus.

I sincerely believed that that would be all the reward we should receive for our campaign in the New World. I can truly declare that I had never even jotted down the amount of my pay as an officer in the service of Congress. I was wrong in my belief, however, and found out afterwards that I had lost nothing by fighting for honest people.

After several years of an active life a state of peace seemed very irksome to me. I went from Paris to my regiment, and from my regiment to Paris. I thought of resuming the study of mathematics, and found a professor. I shall always remember with pleasure the quiet and modest M. Pinel * who taught me mathematics. He had hung up his doctor's hat, and never carried a gold-headed cane when he came to give me my lessons. I was surprised to learn some years afterwards that the celebrated Dr. Pinel and my former professor of mathematics were one and the same person.

Not wishing to make my living by it, I would not

* See Note J.

study mathematics all my life, and the days were long, especially to one who had vowed, as I have already said, not to gamble. I therefore resolved to learn the violin, and in my case, tastes soon become passions, and the dominant one for the time being drives out all the others. After glory had come mathematics, and after mathematics came the violin. I devoted myself entirely to the instrument, with an ardour which now I find it difficult to understand and took lessons from all the great professors of the day. I was the pupil of Capron, Jarnowiek, Traversa, and Viotti. I could perform the most difficult concertos, but I question if I could have played a jig or a country dance with half the dash and spirit shown by many a village carpenter.

Thus did I pass my winters at Paris at the house of my respected uncle, President de Salaberry, dividing my time between arts and social intercourse. The six remaining months I spent in garrison, going from the stables to parade, and from parade to the exercise ground. The silken thread of my life was smooth and even, but I felt a longing for adventures, and at one time I really believed there was a chance of my getting some fighting in India.

One of the missionary priests brought to Paris a youth whom he called the pretender to the throne of Cochin-China. This young Tonkinese prince— whose legitimate claim to the throne I never for an instant doubted—had in his suite several mandarins, who were the smallest men I ever saw, and the young prince himself did not give promise of being any taller. In fact it was difficult to look at them without laughing. The report given by the reverend father, and our commercial interests, half induced the Government to help the little prince to regain his throne, all the force that he required to effect this being a couple of frigates, and some 500 soldiers. I was told that Comte de Béhague, who commanded at Belle-Isle would be the head of the expedition. I knew him very well, and I hastened to beg him to solicit the Minister to give me a command under the Comte in this expedition. I was in error, there had never been any question of employing Comte de Béhague, and I do not know to whom the command was eventually given.

It was a pleasant dream the more; but at all events I had the advantage of seeing the royal present which the little prince had bestowed,—I do not know why,—on the Comtesse la Marck. She was then living in the Tuileries, in the rooms now occupied by the Dauphiness. I saw on the chimney-piece a pair of stag's horns,—a singular present about which a good many sarcastic remarks were made. For my own part, I was more struck by the beauty of the Cochin-Chinese stags than I was by the importance of a kingdom, the sovereign of which could be driven from his throne by five hundred men and a couple of frigates, but, between ourselves, I never said this until after I knew that I should not belong to the expedition.

This dislike to repose, and uneasy longing for war, or rather this undefined need of activity and love of change is characteristic of the French, and I was not the only person to suffer from it. It was a fever which affected, in one way or other, all ranks of society, at this epoch.

Louvois,* it is said, declared war against the Palatinate because he had contradicted his master on a question concerning one of the windows at Trianon, when the King was right, and he was wrong. Ever since the American war, the heads of all the youths of the court and the city had been in a state of ferment. Imitation was all the rage, and the English and Americans,—the two most thoughtful, practical, and solid nations in the world,—were held up as models to be imitated by the most witty and frivolous people. To this strange infatuation was joined also that discontented grumbling spirit peculiar to the French. The government should have provided the people with some object,—no matter what it was,—to distract their attention. Were not duels fought about the relative merits of Gluck and Piccini, for want of other motives? A pretext should have been found to take up the quarrel of the Stadtholder and Holland, and defend the United Provinces against Prussia. A war with Prussia would have suited the belligerent instincts of our impulsive and over numerous youths, and would have served to retard the advent of that

* See Note K.

terrible drama called the French Revolution by at least ten years. More than this even should have been done, and when England was in a dangerous situation owing to her struggle with her revolted colonies, France should have acted as mediator, and not as an auxiliary to the other side. We should have recovered Canada, Spain, and Gibraltar; nor would there have been much difficulty (in mediating), for in the Congress of the thirteen States, six members, including Washington himself, voted against a rupture with the mother country;—but it was decreed on high that it was not to be so.

I am sure that about this time,—either in 1785, or 1786—I forget which year and month,—I read in the *Mercure* the following prophecy.

INSCRIPTION FOUND AT LISKA, IN HUNGARY, ON THE TOMB OF REGIO MONTANUS.

Post mille expletos à partu Virginis annos
Et septigenos rursùs abindè datos,
Octogesimus octavus mirabilis annus
Ingruet et secum tristia fata feret.
Si non hoc anno totus malus occidet orbis,
Si non in nihilum terra fretumque ruent,
Cuncta tamen mundi rursum ibant atque deorsum
Imperia et luctus undique grandis erit. *

---

* A thousand years after the birth of our Lord, and seven hundred years more, the eighty-eighth, a memorable year, will come, and bring sad events. If this year the wicked world is not destroyed,—if the sea and the land are not brought to nothing,—all thrones will be again overturned, and universal mourning shall prevail.

I am aware that Regio Montanus, or Muller died at Rome in 1476, and was buried in the Pantheon. He was not, I believe, a prophet any more than Nostradamus was, but, whether there is an error in the place of his burial, or whether the verses are falsely ascribed to him, is beside the question. I saw them and read them in the *Mercure*, in 1785, 86, or 87, and in 1788 the political atmosphere of France and all Europe was disturbed by violent storms, and the verses were reprinted in all the French and foreign papers. I make no remarks thereon, but content myself with noting the coincidence. To the year 1788 succeeded 1789, when the Revolution burst forth,—a calamity of which no one calculated the extent, and for the results of which we have had to pay dearly.

Amongst the enthusiasts were those infatuated with the novel ideas they had imbibed in the classic ground of America, and joined to them were the young lords of the Court who were associated with some literary men, and thought themselves very clever because they frequented the society of the witty and impertinent Champfort. He laughed at them, and with good reason. He it was who once, on a yacht on the Moerdick, impudently said to the Comte de Narbonne and the Comte de Choiseul, "My dear friends, do you know of anything in the world more idiotic than a French gentleman!"

To these were joined the disciples of that school, the head-quarters of which were the Hotel de la

Rochefoucauld, in the Rue de Seine, presided over by Madame d'E——, the members of which comprised philosophers, philanthropists, economists, —all the grumblers; the Vicomte de B——, who was nothing at all, except a good dancer; and Le C——, a little monkey of an Abbé, crooked as Scarron, but remarkable for turbulent oratory. The Queen sarcastically called him General Jocko. There was also Heraut-de-Sechelles, * a social favourite, who could have attained the highest posts in the magistracy without the trouble of saying or doing anything, for he enjoyed the interest and goodwill of everybody, and had some wit, and, it was said, talent. He was related to Madame de Polignac, and openly protected by the Queen of France. So much for the city.

As to the court, it may well be asked what spirit of insanity had seized all the admirers and votaries of constitutional system and revolutionary ideas, and in fact all these reformers *à talons rouges* † to make them so desirous of a new order of things, and so hungry for any change from the existing order of affairs. Some of them were led astray by a false ambition, and each thought himself, no doubt, called upon to play the part of a second Washington. Such, I imagine, was the case of the two L——'s, the nephews of the Maréchal de R——, both of them in favour with the Queen,

* See Note L.
† The courtiers. It was a mark of nobility to wear shoes with red heels. ED.

who had bestowed upon each a regiment. These Court revolutionists, anxious to ingratiate themselves with the mob, displayed the blackest ingratitude, and their mountebank endeavours to obtain popularity and pose as philanthropists, made them resemble the dog who dropped the meat for the shadow.

Some of them were credulous enough to imagine that if a Revolution did come, it could be stopped at exactly the right point to suit their personal interests.

The Duc d'Orléans and his friends thought that the Revolution would turn out to their advantage by causing a change in the dynasty, but they could not foresee that, if the King came to the scaffold, they also would go there, either before him, with him, or after him.

The Parliaments thought themselves sure of the good opinion of the people because they had refused to support the stamp act and the land tax, and because they had demanded "States General."

The moneyed classes of Paris were in favour of the Revolution ever since M. Vernier had told them that the Nation would take the public debt under its special care;—they were painfully undeceived when the same man said two years later that he would make two-thirds of them bankrupt.

The only persons who were not under a delusion were those who having nothing to lose had everything to gain, and the majority of them were but raised to be dashed down again.

Whatever anyone was bold enough to do he could do with impunity, as far as the monarchy was concerned. Louis XVI, the best natured and most honest man in his kingdom, said to his reader, M. de Septchênes, who had been reading to him the history of the English Revolution in 1641, "If I had been in the place of Charles I, I would never have drawn my sword against my people."

That excellent prince should never have said that or even thought it. On 23rd June 1789, the King, addressing the States General, said, "Gentlemen, I command you to adjourn at once." The King left, and President Bailly remained. Mirabeau replied to M. de Brézé, who had repeated the king's order, "Go and tell your Master that we are here by the will of the people, and will not depart till we are driven out by bayonets." From that moment the Revolution was proclaimed.

All the events, crimes, misfortunes, and excesses which rapidly followed were but the inevitable consequences of these first acts, and therefore I will not dwell here upon the 14th July, and all the awful scenes of that terrible day.

Animus meminisse horret luctuque refugit.

The establishment of the National Guard at Paris to keep the insurrection within bounds, was deemed a sacred duty, but by that very act the Royal power was suspended, and, from that day, France had twelve hundred legislators, of whom the Empress Catharine II said, that "No one would obey them, except the King." It was not the King, it was not the so-called National Assembly, it was the people, who, on 16th July, appointed M. Bailly Mayor of Paris, and M. de la Fayette, Commander of the National Guard.

The same day,—16th July,—the Comte d'Artois, the House of Condé, and Prince de Conti, left France, and the emigration commenced.

M. de la Fayette was then Commander of the Paris Militia, and the General Fairfax of the French Revolution. Many proposals were made to me to join my old comrades in arms, and serve under the orders of this general. My attachment to him was not so great that I felt forced to follow him in any path which it seemed right to him to take, and I refused. It has been wisely said that, in a time of revolution, to *do* your duty is not so difficult as to *know* your duty. I knew mine, and I did it; I should have acted the same could I have foreseen future events. The worst of all positions is to be between the hammer and the anvil, which in France, at that time, meant to be between the Revolution and the Monarchy. A choice had to be made. It appeared to me that I could best assist the cause of the Monarchy by emigrating; to many other people,— and I do not blame them,—it appeared that it could best be helped by their staying in France; some of them, indeed, could not do otherwise. I will not discuss the matter; thousands of pages might be written and the question still remain unsolved, or further than ever from a solution. I wish to narrate here only personal events and circumstances memories teeming with observations that may be useful to others beside myself.

My brother and I emigrated, being both persuaded, —as were all the émigrés who formed the Prince's army—that we might inscribe on our banners, "*Veni, vidi, vici,*" and we entered Champagne in 1792 with the King of Prussia.

Verdun was captured 3rd September, and the next day the army could and should have arrived at Chalons, which is only thirty leagues from Paris, where King Louis XVI and his family were then prisoners in the Temple. The French army, inferior to us in numbers, covered an immensely long line, and would not have been able to stop the eighty thousand men commanded by the Duke of Brunswick, from reaching Paris. But not a day should have been lost, and we lost whole weeks.

The war of 1792 was but a war of Cabinet intrigues, fallacious negotiations, false calculations, in which each of the powers was misled, and the cause of the French Princes, the Bourbon Monarchy, and the unfortunate Louis XVI and his family counted for nothing. The Revolutionists alone were the only persons not deceived and misled, and they won the campaign without having to fight.

In this famous campaign of 1792, commanded

by the first General in Europe, the celebrated Crown Prince, having under his orders 60,000 Prussians with the King of Prussia, and 20,000 Frenchmen with the King's brothers, both armies might have said that they never saw the enemy. A few skirmishes with outposts or with the advance guard were dignified by the Revolutionists into battles and victories. They were right, for these skirmishes were the only visible result of the war, and in fact all this invincible armament accomplished was the capture of Verdun. The magistrates presented Frederick with the keys of the town, and some confectioners' girls brought some anisette,—an attention for which they paid dearly, for the ferocious Jacobins afterwards sent these unoffending persons to the scaffold. The Duke of Brunswick capitulated, retired, and repassed the frontier, to the indignation of the French princes and the 20,000 armed men who had followed them; to the disgust of all true soldiers,—men like General Clairfait;—and to the astonishment of all France and the Jacobins themselves, for the mob will never learn this eternal truth, that great events spring from the most trivial causes, and even from the lowest and most absurd motives.

Proh! pudor! A retreat was ordered in accordance with the capitulations, but the French hussars plundered the baggage of our rear guard. A dull grey sky, continual rain, mud in which horses sank to their bellies, and wagon wheels to the hub, were the sinister omens which accompanied our retrograde march. Add to these also the complaints and consternation of the inhabitants, who had indiscreetly welcomed us on our triumphant entrance, and who now feared to remain exposed to the vengeance of the bloodthirsty ruffians whose fury would know no bounds.

Entire families of Alsatians followed the army in its retreat. Many indeed still remained under the yoke, and after the fatal day which ended the campaign of 1792 by a shameful and inexplicable retreat, it is difficult to say which were the more unfortunate, those French people who left their country or those who remained there. In France nearly every family was devastated by death, which fell upon people of every rank and every age.

From the 10th August 1792, until 9th Thermidor 1794, no citizen, though he belonged to the temporarily dominant faction, was sure that he would sleep another night in his bed, and that he would not be led to the prison and the scaffold.

Outside France, after the retreat from Champagne, all the French *émigrés* and their families may be said, generally speaking, to have made shipwreck of their hopes and prospects. Happy were they who found a place of refuge, and a stone on which they could lay their head. Europe did not suffice to accommodate these restless wanderers, as I discovered for myself when my good fortune caused me again to cross the ocean and revisit North America ten years later. That visit was not the least curious of my experiences, but I must not anticipate events.

All the cleverest, coolest, and most thoughtful men in the army which entered France, had calculated that the campaign would be over in a fortnight. Many peasants had emigrated with the gentlemen of their province, or the officers of their regiment. With the exception of the engineers, every branch of the services was well represented, for a great part of the artillery, nearly the whole of the naval, and a large majority of the infantry and cavalry officers, had responded to the appeal of the King's brothers, the Prince de Condé, and Marshals de Broglie and de Castries.

The retreat, which almost resembled a rout, had undeceived even the most confident of us. In France, all *émigrés* were proscribed under pain of death, so everyone who had a family to protect or support sought for a haven of safety and rest. My brother and I reached Switzerland, and stayed, in turn, on the shores of the Lake of Geneva, at Lausanne, and in the Canton of Vaud.

My brother, who was by nature the most calm, thoughtful and least adventurous man in the world, had so completely shared in the general error as to the certainty of our success, that he had contributed all his available cash, amounting perhaps to 40,000 francs, to the fund, raised at Coblentz by the gentlemen of our province, for the support of the army. He entered on the campaign with fifty pieces of gold in his pocket, and a horse worth eighty louis under him. When we arrived at Basle, we found ourselves in poverty. We had no servant, and carried what property we had about us; we could have appropriately quoted the saying of Bias;* so my brother was obliged to sell his horse in order to save its keep, and the Bucephalus of eighty louis was sold for twenty-five. I should not have noted this incident but for a curious remark that it recalls to my recollection. A long time afterwards my brother was recounting his adventures to some of his Swiss friends, who were listening with interest and attention to the recital of his political and pecuniary difficulties. When he mentioned the sale of a valuable horse at such a low price, a worthy Swiss, thinking only of himself, said with native simplicity, "You should have kept that bargain for me." He was a good honest fellow, for if he had not been, he would not have been capable of making such a very naïve remark.

The Revolutionary storm had extended over all France, and covered the entire horizon, but we believed that it was but a storm, and we must put up with what we could not prevent, and whilst the evil days endured, the best thing to be done was to find a shelter for myself and family in some hospitable land.

---

* One of the "seven sages" of Greece. When his native town was taken by an enemy, the inhabitants saved all they could, and advised Bias, who bore no burden, to follow their example. "I am doing so," said he, "for I carry my all valuables with me."

We did not foresee, or consequently fear, that the Revolutionary party would confiscate and sell the property of all absentees, without distinction of rank, age, or sex. This compelled my sister-in-law and her two sons to join us. She left the Château of Pontgibaud, in which she had resided since the rather recent death of our father. He died some months before the Revolution broke out, and was, at least, spared the pain of seeing it. My sister-in-law had left all her furniture in the manor-house, and the keys, so to speak, in the doors, for she thought she was only going to be absent a short time. The utmost that she expected was that the estates would be sequestrated for a short period. She brought with her therefore, as little baggage as possible, in order to experience the less difficulty in passing the frontier, but fortunately brought her jewel-case, which in this hour of misfortune, became the means of saving us all.

The family consisted of my brother, his wife, their two sons,—the one a youth, the other a young child,—a lady's maid who had insisted on following her mistress, and a musician, named Monsieur Leriche, a man whose talents were only surpassed by his good qualities.

A consultation was held as to the best means of gaining a livelihood, and the plan agreed upon was strictly followed. Adversity is the touchstone of resolute minds, and men of resolution rarely fail to win in the long run. My brother and his wife afford an instructive and encouraging example of what can be done by a father and a mother having united aims, and trust in God and in their own efforts. To vanquish evil fortune, they called in the aid of resignation, courage, employment, and perseverance, and joined to those qualities, foresight, economy, and natural, or acquired, aptitude.

It is with admiration mingled with respect that I think of their continual labour day and night, and its gradually widening results, and that I remember the more or less fortunate attempts, which marked the reconstruction of my brother's fortune. Though he had possessed rich estates, and houses in Paris, he had lost all, and his total resources, in a strange country, did not amount to more than ten thousand francs.

But he and his wife had the patience and perseverance of beavers, which when their huts have been carried away by a flood, immediately set to work to re-construct them. They began to work for their own living, and that of their family. My brother, who when he was rich had cultivated for his own pleasure his taste for the arts and sciences, now utilized his acquirements as adjuncts to the business he was trying to found. Drawing, mechanics, chemistry, agriculture, mineralogy, and mathematics,—he had studied all; and he found or made opportunities to employ all his knowledge.

I cannot, without emotion, and without feeling faith in that Providence which has said, "Aid yourself and I will aid you," think of this tiny rill of water which became a rolling river of Pactolus, these small efforts which in ten years developed into a thriving industry. To the praise of human nature let it be said, that from the very beginning of his industrial and commercial scheme, his courage, perseverance, imperturbable coolness, honesty, exactitude in fulfilling all his engagements, and his constant schemes, as prudent as they were ingenious, met with that support and good-will which a man who possesses these qualities will alway obtain.

My sister-in-law, though but just before she had been accustomed to all the enjoyments and luxuries of life, or rather to the honourable use of wealth, became in twenty-four hours a housekeeper, and worked with her own hands. She could embroider, and her faithful maid was also of use to her in this work. Her husband had become an artist, and invented designs in embroidery which he sold for a crown each, or sometimes the women worked them. When he had again become a millionaire, I have heard my brother,—who was as quiet and unassuming in his manners in his prosperity as he had been in adversity,—when he went, as he often did, to see Comte de C——, who comes from our province, and is our friend and neighbour, always ask to see N——, the Comte's old valet. N—— had formerly been a small tradesman at Lausanne, and had ordered patterns from my brother and paid him a crown each for them, to the mutual satisfaction of both parties. Such is the way of the world. Whilst the women and my brother worked, our fellow boarder, M. Leriche, the musician, would give concerts in the different towns in Switzerland, and bring back the pecuniary results of his tour,—the harmonious sounds of his Stradivarius converted by our Amphion into ducats,—as his contribution to the common fund. He insisted upon paying all the school expenses of my young nephew.

"Did you not give me a pension, Monsieur le Comte, when you were rich?" said the kind-hearted, honest musician when he first joined our little household. "It is bad enough that you have lost your fortune, there is no need you should lose your friend as well. As for the pension, let it go: you can renew it some day, when we have returned to France." My other nephew, being older, was serving in Condé's army.

At any rate the manufacture prospered, being further helped by some new workmen, also *émigrés*, being some of the officers of the regiment my brother had commanded, and whom he had sent for and informed that he could find them means to live honourably by the work of their own hands. The calamities and excesses at Lyon brought to L—— a number of merchants, who had managed to save between them a large quantity of merchandise, and, before long, my brother enjoyed their good opinion and confidence.

It was proposed to him he should visit the great fairs of Leipzig and Frankfort, and sell goods on commission. Being quick and clever, as well as scrupulously honest, he was fortunate in all his transactions in every journey. He obtained credit, by the aid of which he was able to do business for himself. He sent embroidery even into Italy, and also took the productions of his own workshops to Frankfort and Leipzig. He even did some business in diamonds, having acquired in earlier days, some knowledge of precious stones. Thus he reaped where he had sown, and was able to turn to advantage the varied knowledge he had gained in his youth.

I heard one day that the Americans, who were increasing in prosperity year by year, were now in a condition to pay their back debts, and had decided that all officers who had fought in the War of Independence should upon presentation, receive all their pay with interest to date. To me this was a real *peculium adventilium*, for I had long since given up all hopes of ever seeing any of that money. I was glad to learn that there was a sum at my disposal, and without loss of time started for Hamburg to embark on the first vessel ready to sail for North America.

I found an American three-master of good appearance, for they had, and justly, the reputation of being very good ship builders, but, as there was not at that time any Admiralty supervision in the

United States, many vessels were lost at sea through the rashness or carelessness of the sailors. I was mistaken; the ship had been newly painted, and the paint hid the faults, but the first rough weather we experienced showed me that she was worthless. I made a remark to this effect to the captain, and was not much reassured to find he agreed with me. He coolly remarked that he thought she would manage to reach the other side, but in any case it would be her last voyage. Nevertheless we entered the Delaware without meeting with any accident, and the tide being in our favour, I landed at Philadelphia

CHAPTER VI.

My third voyage to the United States—Philadelphia transformed into a new Sidon—The same simplicity of manners—Mr. MacHenry, Secretary of War—M. Duportail—Moreau de Saint-Mery—I meet my old friends again—A triple partnership with Senator Morris at the head of it—Burke's prophecy—Plans proposed to me—Viscount Noailles—The Bishop of Autun—A mission to the Directory to claim an indemnity—Marino, the pastry-cook, and M. de Volney—The Princes of Orléans—An elephant with a French driver—A trip to New York.—Colonel Hamilton—Past, present, and future of the United States—I meet the Chevalier de la C——Our recollections of M. de la Fayette—His escape from the fortress of Olmutz.—Dr. Bollman—My return to Europe and arrival at Hamburg.

I HAD fully expected that six years of peace and stability would have repaired the ravages done by the long war, and that those houses which threatened to fall in ruins would have been repaired, for during the war, want of resources prevented the State from undertaking anything, the needs of the army absorbing all the money—but I was far from expecting the magic and magnificent spectacle which the first rays of the sun showed me.

It was not a rebuilt, restored, plastered over Philadelphia that I saw, but a new Thebes, a new Sidon. The port teemed with war ships, or merchant ships, equipped or in construction; on the quays there were a thousand new houses, and public buildings which resembled palaces,—an Exchange in marble, the United States Bank, Congress Hall, all showed me that Philadelphia had become in six years, populous, flourishing, industrious, rich, and powerful.

But if I did not recognize the city, I did the inhabitants—the natives, I mean. As to the strangers who formed a floating population, I could not help smiling as I noted some faces I had seen elsewhere, but I will speak of them later on, they ought to have a chapter to themselves.

My first care was to see after the principal object of my voyage, the recovery of my pay and the back interest on it, for my surprise and admiration at the city did not make me forget the business I had come upon. The account being made up it seemed there was due to me about 50,000 francs, but the papers which would enable me to claim the sum were in Paris. In default of these papers it was necessary that two householders should be surety for me. I knew a good many old officers, but none of them possessed sufficient means to be accepted as bail for me. The President of the United States, General Washington himself, was kind enough to relieve me from this embarrassment, and the 50,000 francs were paid over to me, and placed to my account.

The object of my mission being fulfilled, the

remainder of my stay at Philadelphia until my return to Europe, was employed in the observations of an idle traveller with an unfettered and philosophic mind.

The Government officials were as simple in their manners as ever. I had occasion to call upon Mr. MacHenry, the Secretary of War. It was about eleven o'clock in the morning when I called. There was no sentinel at the door, all the rooms, the walls of which were covered with maps, were open, and in the midst of this solitude I found two clerks, each sitting at his own table, engaged in writing. At last I met a servant, or rather *the* servant, for there was but one in the house, and asked for the Secretary. He replied that his master was absent for the moment, having gone to the barber's to be shaved. Mr. MacHenry's name figured in the State Budget for $2000 (10,500 francs) a salary quite sufficient in a country where the Secretary for War goes in the morning to his neighbour, the barber at the corner, to get shaved.

I was as much surprised to find all the business of the War Office transacted by two clerks, as I was to hear that the Secretary had gone to the barber's; both details were in harmony with the spirit of a nation that knew how to pay its debts. This recalls to my mind the very singular recompense which the American Congress awarded to General Stark, the conqueror of Burgoyne.

The British general, dressed in a magnificent

uniform, covered with gold lace, and with a cocked hat on his head, had been obliged to surrender his sword to General Stark, who for his part, wore an old blanket for a cloak, had a cotton cap stuck over one ear, and thick, heavy shoes on his feet. It was a typical representation of a poor and oppressed people triumphing over a rich and insolent monarchy. Congress, in a sudden accession of generosity, ordered that the conqueror should be presented with two ells of blue, and one of yellow, cloth to make him a coat, and half a dozen shirts of Dutch linen.

I well remember hearing General Stark complain loudly in my presence, when he received this gift of the nation, that Congress had forgotten to give him any cambric to make the cuffs.

This fact, which in the present day would appear incredible, was made the subject of endless jokes in the English papers of the day, then ready enough to find any subject on which they could twit the conquerors.

What curious reflections this antique simplicity suggests, especially when we consider that even now, thirty-five years afterwards, the same principles prevail. What will become of effete old Europe with its budgets of thousands of millions, when compared to a Republic governed so cheaply, that the Government appears to be done by contract, where even the President is obliged to represent the nation on a salary of 125,000 francs, and is the only man allowed to have a sentinel at his door?

Mr. MacHenry, the Secretary of War, recalled to my mind the name of a French ex-Minister of War, my old comrade, M. Duportail. I learned that my old friend was still in the United States, and that he had bought a little farm near the city, so I hastened to call upon him. I met him at a little distance from his house, and, judge of my astonishment, or rather inclination to laugh, at finding him dressed in full French fashion, with his hat under his arm, though he was eighteen hundred leagues from Paris. It was ten years since the Revolution broke out, but he appeared to be still awaiting the news that his portfolio had been restored to him. That was his daily and hourly thought,—a hobby as innocent as that of Uncle Toby,—and after he had expressed his pleasure at seeing me again, his conversation was of nothing but the ingratitude of the French nation, and the admirable projects for the improvement of the army that he had intended to carry out.

"Ah," he said, "how sorry I was to hear you had emigrated. What a fine chance of promotion you would have had if you had remained with us. You had been through the war in America, and, when I was Minister, I would have given you whatever you asked for."

That would have been easy enough for him, it is true, but, all other considerations apart, his present condition was not calculated to make me regret the step I had taken, for all that remained to his Excellency of all his former grandeur,—which had lasted but six months,—was a little farm in the New World, a couple of leagues from the primæval forests, and within three days' journey of the borders of civilization.

But his fall, which appeared to him so impossible, and such a political mistake, was no more of a fortuitous circumstance than his rise, which he could never have expected either.

Alas, I met in the streets of Philadelphia plenty of great men brought down to the dust again, men whose ambition had deceived them, fools punished for their folly, men of yesterday who were no longer men of to-day, and *parvenus* astonished to find that Fortune's wheel had not stood still when they were uppermost.

For my private instruction, my friend Duportail told me the names of the French refugees who had found in Philadelphia an ark of safety like that of Noah. The blowing up of the good ship, the French Monarchy, had been caused by their follies and mistaken notions, and the explosion had thrown a good number of them over to the United States. But they were not corrected or disabused of their errors, and brought to a better state of mind, but each and all,—Constitutionalists, Conventionalists, Thermidorians, Fructidorians,—imagined that their political downfall had been brought about by some ill-chance just as their plans were within an ace of succeeding. They kept their eyes fixed on France, to which they all expected to return sooner on later and recommence what each called his *great work*, for there were exactly the same number of political systems as there were refugees. In the United States you might have believed yourself in the Elysian Fields described in the Sixth Book of the Æneid, where the shades still pursue the same ideas they had cherished in the other world.

But a man must live, and the most curious spectacle was to see these Frenchmen, fallen from their former greatness, and now exercising some trade or profession.

One day I entered a shop to buy some pens and paper, and found the proprietor to be Moreau de Saint-Méry,* one of the famous "electors" of the Hotel de Ville, of Paris, in 1789.

"You do not know, I suppose," he said pompously, when I had finished making my purchases, "who I am and what I was?"

"No, upon my life, I do not," I replied.

"Well," he said, "I,—the very man you see before you,—was ruler of Paris for three days, and now I am obliged to sell pens, ink, and paper, in Philadelphia, to gain a living."

I was not so much surprised at this fresh instance of the instability of human affairs as I was to find this *petit bourgeois* really believe that he should astonish posterity. Nor was I particularly astonished

* See Note M.

either to learn, some months later, that he was a bankrupt, but I may remark that he failed for twenty-five thousand francs, and I would not have given a thousand crowns for all the stock in M. Moreau de Saint-Méry's shop. Strange to say there is no country where bankruptcy is so frequent;— every morning you see sales by auction in some of the streets.

A good many other personages besides "the electors of 1789," and who when in France, had cut quite another figure, were to be found walking about the streets of Philadelphia, as the Vicomte de Noailles, Duc de L——, M. S——, Volney, the Bishop of Autun, and *tutti quanti*.

Some of them gambled on the Stock Exchange, and nearly always successfully. Others were not so fortunate, and their speculations were more risky; nor were they above laying traps for those of their countrymen who had newly arrived in America.

Senator Morris had conceived a vast and adventurous undertaking. The celebrated Burke had written somewhere or other that Europe was about to totally collapse, and that North America was destined to receive the refugees and all the goods they were able to save. The Senator, in company with M. S—— and Vicomte de Noailles, speculated on this prophecy. They acquired more than a million acres, situated on the banks of the Susquehannah, and this land, divided into large or small lots, was advertised in the papers under the heading of " Good land to be sold." Nothing was said about residences—the purchaser was apparently to build his house to suit his own taste. To encourage their clients they also constructed in the city an immense building in which all the great personages they were expecting on the faith of Edmund Burke could be suitably lodged. The Pope, the Sacred College, a few dethroned monarchs, and other notables, were to rest there till they had recovered from the effects of their sea voyage, and before making up their minds to purchase a slice of American territory.

It is literally true that this enterprising company had agents on the look-out for all emigrants who arrived from Europe. Their factotums kept a watchful eye on all newly-landed passengers, who appeared to have some baggage, and not only compassionated their misfortunes, but offered them the means of repairing their loss, by the purchase, in a new and hospitable land, of another estate of dimensions proportionate to the means of each new-comer. The price was reasonable enough,—only six francs an acre,—but the agent did not say that it had cost the Company he represented only fifteen cents an acre.

I knew a milliner who had made some money, and who purchased an estate at Asylum, the fictitious capital of this imaginary colony. The poor dupe went to inspect the estate which she had bought the right to build on, cultivate, and live upon—and then she came back to Philadelphia to gain her living with her ten fingers as she had previously done.

One of these agents, who had not much more sense than the devil of Papefigue, was ill-advised enough to apply to me, having heard, perhaps, some vague rumours about my being a French *émigré* and possessing some money. He did not trouble to enquire where that money came from, and how I had gained it, but started at once with a long discourse on the principles of humanity which animated this philanthropic enterprise, and then went on to boast of the beauty of situation, the fertility of the soil, the rich prairies to be mowed, etc. "All materials are at hand," he said, "and everything has been provided. There is a master builder paid by the Company. We have even a restaurant in order to spare trouble to our newly-arrived colonists." He strongly urged me to buy five hundred acres of this new Promised Land—all for the modest sum of a thousand crowns.

I took care not to interrupt him, and let him persuade himself that he had convinced me, and that I believed his statements, but when he had finished I told him that there was not a stone in the whole country, that two hundred acres of that land would not support a cow, and that no meat was to be found there unless you killed a deer. I added that as I had been all through the War of Independence I knew all about the district he had been describing, and that his boasted philanthropic speculation was a mockery and a snare. I ended by saying that the last and worst misfortune which could befall the unfortunate French emigrants, was to find themselves swindled by their own countrymen—men heartless enough to impose upon the credulity of strangers, and sell them a few sandhills planted with scrub-pine for an Eldorado.

I have never seen a man look more disconcerted than this unlucky agent did, but I should like to have seen the reception that the speculative triumvirate—to whom I had the honour to be known—gave their clumsy emissary when he rendered an account of his visit.

Providence, however, did not permit the enterprise to succeed, and the three speculators came to a bad end. Senator Morris, crippled with debts, died in prison; M. T—— went mad, and Vicomte de Noailles,* after having won four or five hundred thousand francs on the Philadelphia Exchange, left for St. Domingo, where he was killed on board an English cruiser. He, at least, died like a brave man, as he had lived;—that much praise is due to his memory, but that does not prevent me from relating a story concerning him which is a proof the more of the inconsistency displayed by some of our illustrious *faiseurs* during the Revolution. The incident occurred under my own eyes, and I laughed heartily at it, as everybody else did.

This ex-Vicomte had a deed drawn up at Philadelphia by one of the notaries of the city, and when it was read over to him, he perceived that he was

* See Note N.

mentioned therein by the name of M. de Noailles. He was exceedingly angry at this, and insisted that the deed should be re-written and none of his titles forgotten—Vicomte, Knight of Saint Louis, Knight of Malta, etc. The next day, the newspapers were impertinent enough to repeat—*con licinza superiori* —what had passed in the office, and all Philadelphia knew of the quarrel of the Vicomte with his notary. The story was accompanied by a note to this effect: "It is singular that a member of the Constitutional Assembly, who proposed the law of *ci-devants*,—a French nobleman who, on the famous night of 4th August made a holocaust of the titles, deeds, armorial bearings, etc., of all the nobility, commencing with his own,—should insist on those titles being applied to him in a land of political equality, where all distinctions are unknown."

Let us pass on to another *émigré*. The Bishop of Autun,* who had been requested to "get out" of England, had established himself in the free land of America. Monseigneur wore a pigtail and would willingly have said as Abbé Raynal did, "When I was a priest." He was not at all troubled about his present condition, and still less about his future; he speculated, and laughed at everything and everybody. His company was much sought after, for he was an amusing companion and had plenty of wit of his own, though many witticisms of other persons were often ascribed to him.

* See Note O.

In spite of all his wit and amiability he was looked upon somewhat coolly by the best society of Philadelphia, with whom his light, careless manners did not meet with the welcome they deserved. In fact the Anglo-Americans are simple and straightforward in their manners, and the cynical, irreverent contempt of their guest for all things Americans respected greatly scandalized them. M. de Talleyrand had the right, if it pleased him, to pull off his clerical gown and trail it in the mud, but he had also at that time a position as a French *émigré*, and though he might resign for himself the welcome bestowed upon unfortunate people in that position, he also indirectly injured others. Were the Americans right to be vexed with his conduct? Everyone may judge for himself.

Cardinal de Richelieu, when he went at night to visit Marion de Lorme, was careful to disguise himself as a cavalier, with spurs on his boots, yet he did not escape being ridiculed. The Bishop of Autun did not take these precautions, having peculiar ideas as to the rights of man, and confidence in the unbounded liberty to be found in the New World. He might be seen walking the streets of Philadelphia, in open day, with a coloured woman on his arm. This was a gratuitous insult to the manners and customs which—rightly or wrongly—prevail in the country, and where social prejudices have such weight and importance that not even an ensign of hussars would dare to run counter to them.

The Americans were certainly accustomed to see Quakers, who would not take off their hats, and even shirtless savages; but all, from the Congressman, to the workman, read one or other of the thousands of newspapers which appeared, and they were not ignorant of the celebrity and the responsible position of M. de Talleyrand. All the details of his life as a priest were known, from the first act of it,—his installation as Bishop of Autun,—to the last, when he officiated at the Altar of the Country in the Champ de Mars on the famous day of the Federation of 1790. A refugee so celebrated should have exercised some circumspection in regard to his private life.

That he did not preserve his ecclesiastical character when he was outside the pale of the Catholic, Apostolic, and Roman Church, the following story will testify. M. de Talleyrand had with him a fierce dog, which was a very sagacious animal. When it wanted to enter its master's house it would ring the bell, and if the door was not opened, instead of waiting it would go to the lady's house, and lie upon the bed until the return of the two lovers.

But instead of relating a part of what the Bishop did, it would be preferable to recall to mind what he told us.

Amongst other things he related, in his own inimitable manner an account of an interview he had at London with a Gascon refugee. Early one morning he heard a knock at his door, and asked, " Who is there?".

"The Chevalier de C——," replied a wheedling voice with a strong accent of the land of the Garonne.

The Bishop of Autun opened the door, and the Chevalier entered and after a series of bows, said, "M. de Talleyrand, I have always heard that you were the cleverest and most sensible man in the world."

M. de Talleyrand imagined that his visitor had come to borrow money, and was ready to reply "I was just going to ask *you*," but it appeared that all the Gascon required was some advice.

"Well, Monsieur, what is it?" asked the Bishop of Autun.

"The fact is, Monsieur de Talleyrand, that I left the manor-house where I lived, and went to Coblentz, and so I am what is called an *émigré*, and now I want to know the best means of getting back to France. As you are so clever will you be kind enough to advise me?"

"What sort of position did you occupy in your province?"

"No position of importance."

"What sort of life did you lead, and what fortune had your family?"

"We are four brothers, and papa has an income of about five thousand francs a year."

"Oh, well, no one is likely to interfere with you. I suppose you have a few crowns left; go to Huninguen, Neufchatel, or Saint Claude. You will be sure to find a guide, some good fellow who will see you across the frontier; then you must avoid all the villages, only travel at night, and as you have the happiness to be unknown, you can reach your 'papa's' house unperceived. Then keep yourself quiet, be wise and discreet; never speak about Coblentz or emigration, and await events."

"Ah, Monsieur de Talleyrand, how grateful I am to you. They were right in saying you are the cleverest man in the world. I will return home to papa; but if a second Revolution should occur, you may bet I will be on the side of the people."

"Take care not to do anything of the kind!" cried Monseigneur. "Take care not to do anything of the kind; next time you might make a mistake."

This last sentence contains quite a characteristic touch, and is the whole point of the anecdote.

The Bishop smiled when he heard of the establishment of the Directory; the diabolical spirit incarnate in him advised him to return to France.

He told us of his intention, and Colonel Hamilton remarked that the country was still in a very disturbed state, whereas in the United States he could live at ease.

"Yes," he said, "but I understand France and the French. Have you never been in a stable when the stable hands have forgotten to give the horses any hay? The horses neigh and stamp."

We on our side represented to him the dangers he ran as a priest, as an emigrant, and finally as *himself.* Any one of these reasons would have sufficed to deter many a brave man, but had no effect on him.

"No," he said laughingly, as he stepped on board the ship which was to take him back, "I have nothing to fear over there; I am up to all the tricks of revolutions."

It was not without difficulty, however, that he could find a vessel to take him. No American captain was willing to give him a passage, perhaps on account of his political importance, or perhaps because he was so much disliked.

In fact, besides the causes I have already mentioned, a report was current that once in a conversation about the loss of Hayti, when someone spoke of the difficulty of reconquering it, and of the scarcity of negroes in America, he said, "Why not establish the slave trade here? The West India Islands are nearer than Africa."

This remark, and the lady of colour, did not tend to place him in the odour of sanctity in Philadelphia. A tempest drove into the Delaware a Prussian ship, and the captain consented to take the ex-Bishop, but the crew did not appear over delighted with their passenger. I should not have been surprised to hear of the sailors doing as they did in an amusing story told by Bacon, when, after having first confessed all their sins to a Capucin monk who was on board, the sailors thought they would appease the wrath of heaven by dropping him into the sea.

Thus we saw depart the *diable boiteux* * who

---

* An accident in infancy had rendered Talleyrand lame for life.

since,—under the name of the Prince de Benevento,—persuaded at the Congress of Vienna the kings of Europe to again march against Bonaparte and, for the second time, put the Bourbons upon the throne of France. *Suum cuique.*

In the pentarchy at the Luxembourg at this time was Citoyen Rewbel, a friend of Citoyen Talleyrand, and immediately upon his arrival our ex-Constitutionalist received from the Jacobin Conventionalist the portfolio of Foreign Affairs.

The worthy Anglo-Americans no sooner learned that their "guest" had become Minister, than they foolishly imagined the occasion and the moment favourable to demand and obtain justice. Forgetting all about the lady of colour, and the proposal to establish the slave trade amongst them, they sent off three members of Congress,—whom I saw go, and return. Their object was to demand compensation in the name of the United States for two hundred merchant vessels flying the American flag, which—*per fas et nefas*—the French Republic had captured during the three years the red cap adorned her brow.

The disappointment and surprise of these ingenuous envoys was worth seeing, when they returned and narrated the details of their mission, and described the kind of diplomats with whom they had come in contact, and the impudence—as they artlessly called it—of the proposals which had been made to them.

The first ambassador was of the feminine sex. A Madame de —— presented herself to the envoys from Congress, described herself as a friend to the cause of the Independence of the United States, which had always been dear to her heart, etc.—and so, having paved the way, announced the visit of the most famous M. R—— de St. F——, who would be able to discuss the affair thoroughly. This second envoy dropped a hint that it was indispensable for the success of the demand that a little money should be spent. The ambassadress then reappeared, and finished by declaring that the affair might be arranged for the sum of fifty thousand livres sterling, of which so much was to go to His Excellency as a *douceur* or "sweetness" (that is the exact word which the Envoys used in their public report to Congress) so much to M. R—— de St. F——, for his part in the negotiations, and so much for "incidental expenses," by which term Madame l'Ambassadrice probably designated her own share of the plunder.

In short, the ambassadors returned with all their evidence and documents—but no money. I was present at the memorable sitting of Congress when one of the envoys read the report he had prepared. There was a mention in it of Citizen Talleyrand, which it is to be hoped he read in the newspapers of the day.

"This man," said the orator, "to whom we have shown the kindest hospitality, is now the Minister of the French Government, and to him we presented ourselves to demand justice. And this guest without gratitude, this Bishop who has renounced his God, was not ashamed to rob us of 50,000 livres; —50,000 livres which went to support his vices!"

I said to myself, "Good, easy people, they are worthy of their country; an Englishman would have found no difficulty in settling the matter."

Many other celebrities of different sorts did I see at Philadelphia during my third sojourn in America, —so different from the two preceding ones. Here is another scene which I saw acted on the same stage, —that is to say in the same city.

Marino, who had formerly been cook to my old friend the Chevalier de Capellis, had, for private and political reasons, taken up his residence in this city, and enjoyed the reputation of being an excellent pastry-cook. One day I was in Marino's shop, ordering some dish,—we were old acquaintances and I knew him to be not only a skilful cook, but a brave and honest fellow,—when a stranger entered. He was unknown to both of us, although he was a Frenchman, and,—as will be seen, --enjoyed some celebrity. The new-comer ordered a *paté*, composed of the choicest delicacies; he was going to invite a score of persons to dinner, and I fancy that the Duc d'Orléan and his brothers were to be amongst the guests. The *paté* was duly ordered, the price was arranged, and all that remained to be done was for the pastry-cook to write down his customer's name and address.

"Volney,"* said the stranger.

"Volney!" roared the cook, who was as great a royalist as his former master, De Capellis,—"Volney! Volney!"

I wish I could have painted him in his wrath, with his white cap on his head, his apron tucked up, and a big knife stuck in his belt. Quitting his stove and its saucepans he came forward, and cried in a voice of thunder,—though his indignation caused it to tremble—

"Get out of here, you scoundrel! Get out of my kitchen, you accursed atheist. You confounded revolutionist, you have robbed me of two-thirds of the money I had invested in Government Stocks. I don't work for"—(I have toned down his remarks)—"people of your kind. My stove shall never get hot for *you*."

And the famous, or too famous, Monsieur Chasseboeuf de Volney had to make his exit from the shop of the best pastry-cook in Philadelphia,—without his *paté*.

I have mentioned that the Princes of Orléans † were to have been present at the dinner at which Marino's *paté* did *not* appear. They had been some time in the country;—they stayed in all about six months. Once, whilst on their way to visit a colonist who lived at some distance from the city, one of the brothers was lost in traversing a forest,

* See Note P.
† See Note Q.

He was found by an Indian, who tracked him as a sleuth-hound would have done.

After some time the Princes of Orléans went South to visit Louisiana, which then belonged to Spain. The Chevalier de Carondelet, who commanded for the King of Spain, received them at New Orleans with all the honours due to their rank; but, during their stay in the United States, no one, —except the French, who, whatever their political opinions might be, could not regard princes of the blood royal of France as ordinary personages,— knew them, saluted them, or designated them but by the name of Equality. To the Americans this appeared the most natural thing in the world. You would read in the newspaper, "Yesterday the Brothers Equality slept at such and such a place," or "We hear from——Town that the Brothers Equality have arrived there."

On one occasion the three princes went to pay a visit to General Washington at Mount Vernon. The negro, who announced them, said to Washington, "Excellency! Excellency! there are three Equalities at the door."

Different countries have different manners.

General Washington received the Princes of Orléans, but his doors were closed against the Vicomte de Noailles, the Bishop of Autun, and even my friend Duportail. The liberator of his country felt deeply for Louis XVI; the King's portrait hung in his room, and he often looked at it, but never without tears in his eyes.

Whilst on this subject I may relate that, during my stay at Philadelphia, an Indian chief was once at dinner in a house where there was a picture of King Louis XVI, after Muller of Stuttgart. Many toasts were proposed, and at last the Indian rose, and standing before the picture, said, to the great astonishment of all the guests, " I drink to the memory of the unfortunate king who was murdered by his subjects."

A number of French persons of both sexes, all ranks, and all opinions, had settled in Philadelphia and New York. Outside each of these cities, and scattered over the eighty miles or so between them, were many colonist who had escaped from the massacres of Hayti and had found refuge. They were in some instances accompanied by negroes who had remained faithful to them. These refugees rented farms between New York and Philadelphia, and having saved their lives, had next to find some means of existence, for living is very dear in this country. The Comtesse de la Tour du Pin had purchased a little farm at Albany, and went to market herself to sell her milk, butter, and poultry: she was much respected by all the country folks.

I remember also that I met an old soldier of the Royal body-guards, who had escaped the massacres of the 5th and 6th October. He had sold a little farm he had in order to buy with the money an elephant, which he had taken the precaution to insure, for in the United States you can insure anything. I was much amused at this novel industry. This soldier of the King's Guards who had left Versailles to become an elephant-driver in North-America, had already had the luck to make fourteen thousand francs by exhibiting his noble animal, which perhaps was a direct descendant of the elephant of King Porus.

Finding myself only some eighty miles from New York, I was curious to revisit the scenes of some of our battles, and also to inspect the city, which I had never seen except from outside, when our army was blockading it. It was with interest and emotion that I revisited Topanah, on the banks of the Akensie River, where the unfortunate Major André was executed. I recognized with more or less pleasure (according to whether they reminded me of victories or defeats) the different positions which our army had successively occupied.

My surprise equalled my curiosity when I entered New York. I admired,—from within this time,—this handsome city, which had then but 25,000 inhabitants (it numbers 120,000 to-day),* and the beautiful neighbouring island called Long Island. I was enchanted with all I saw, the elegance and cleanliness of the houses joined to the beauties of virgin nature; then the width and extent of the water ways, which are almost seas; the giant trees which form the primæval forests of the New World; in fact all which is not the work of men's hands

* In 1828, when the book was written.

is so surprising on account of its imposing and gigantic proportions, that when I returned to Europe I seemed to be in another world—the Continent appeared to me like a pretty miniature reduced from a large picture by means of a pantograph.

I was glad to meet some of my old comrades in arms, both French and Americans; amongst others the brave and wise Colonel Hamilton, the friend of Washington, and who was afterwards unfortunately killed in a duel by Colonel Burgh. Hamilton, who had quitted the army and returned to civil life, was a lawyer, and pleaded in the courts and gave consultations. We often talked together,—much to my profit,—of the causes of the war, the actual condition of the United States, and the probable destiny of the nation. Anyone who had heard us talking about events which were then a matter of history, would have taken us for two of the speakers in Lucian's or Fénélon's "Dialogues of the Dead."

"The American War," I said, "began in a very singular manner, and was carried on in a way yet more singular. It seems to me, on summing up all my observations, that the English made a mistake in sending troops against you, instead of withdrawing those which were already in the country, as you did not submit at once you must have inevitably ended by winning sooner or later. You gained experience and discipline in the indecisive engagements which were fought, and the scholars were bound to finish by becoming as clever as their masters. Look, for instance, at the Swedes under Charles XII, and the Russians under Peter the Great."

"You are right, no doubt," he replied, "but their second fault was to give the two brothers Howe each a command. The general undertook scarcely anything by land in order to allow his brother, the admiral, the chance to distinguish himself at sea. All that the English need have done was to blockade our ports with twenty-five frigates and ten ships of the line. But, thank God, they did nothing of the sort."

"Thank God, indeed," I said, "for I believe that America would have come to terms with the mother country. I am the more inclined to believe this, as I notice there are a great many Tories in your country, and I see that the rich families still cling to the king's government."

"Yes; and thus it happens," he replied, with a smile, "that though our Republic has only been in existence some ten years, there are already two distinct tendencies—the one democratic, the other aristocratic. In Europe they always speak of the American Revolution, but our separation from the mother country cannot be called a revolution. There have been no changes in the laws, no one's interests have been interfered with, everyone remains in his place, and all that is altered is that the seat of government is changed. Real equality exists amongst us at present, but there is a remarkable difference of manners between the inhabitants of the

Northern and Southern States. The negro is free at Philadelphia, but he is a slave in Virginia and Carolina. Large fortunes are made in the Southern States, because the country is rich in productions; but it is not the same in the Northern States."

"Yes," I said, "those who claim to look into the future may see in your nation,—as you say,—two diverging tendencies; the one towards democracy, the other towards aristocracy; but if some separation of these elements could be made quietly and without strife, would the people be any the happier? Territorial possessions are, there is no doubt, but lightly esteemed in your country, which is perhaps owing to the fact that the British or Anglo-Americans of to-day only date back to Penn and his colony, or only a hundred years or so. An estate over here rarely remains ten or twelve years in the same hands."

"That is partly due," answered he, "to the facilities for changing our place of residence, and to the fact that land which is relatively dear near the great cities, is much cheaper at some distance from them. Besides we are essentially business men; with us, agriculture is of small account, commerce is everything."

"That is true," I said. "Many persons believe they have but to land in the United States to make a fortune, and the first question that is put to you when you arrive, is: 'Do you come here to sell or to buy?'"

I have given, as nearly as I can remember it, all that passed between the soldier-lawyer and me at this interview, but I cannot forget the singularly wise reflection that I heard him make one day, on the subject of the French interference in the American War.

"Considering the question by itself," I said to him, "the Cabinet of Versailles would seem to have committed a political fault in having openly supported the Americans in the War of Independence, and more particularly for having sent over here all the young nobility of the Court, who returned embued with republican principles. It has been maintained that the proper action for France was to remain neutral, and take advantage of the difficulties of England, to occupy, and thus make her restore, Canada, which has always remained French at heart. This double opportunity of war, or re-occupation, would have furnished an outlet for surplus population, which, failing that, has overflowed in the form of a revolution on our own monarchy, and has then inundated Europe."

This speech made him think of the young nobles, who had overrun America like the sheep of Panurge, without, however, reducing the surplus population of France, and Colonel Hamilton could not help laughing as he replied:

"You are right. I am speaking in opposition to our own interests, for it is to the French arms that we owe our independence, but your Government would perhaps have done better if it had sent us your lower orders instead of your upper."

I found at Philadelphia, my friend De la Colombe, who, like me, was aide-de-camp to M. de la Fayette during the American War, but with this difference, that when our civil dissensions broke out, he still remained with the general.

"You were wrong, my friend," he said to me, "not perhaps in not casting in your lot with ours, but in refusing on principle to have any communication with us. I might perhaps have been able to dissipate some of your delusions, and induced you to reconsider the matter, and afterwards you could have done as you thought fit."

He told me many things which astonished me, even after the events which I had seen;—especially when he assured me that at the time when we believed all Europe, even including Russia, to be preparing to take up the king's cause by a general armament, Prussia had, through Ephraim, a Jew of Berlin, proposed an offensive and defensive alliance with France, the sole condition being that Louis XVI should send the Queen back to Vienna. I do not refuse to believe that this proposal was really made, but it seems strange that the avowed enemies of this unfortunate Princess should intentionally or unintentionally have tried to save her from the scaffold.

My old comrade of the War of Independence, who had thrown himself, along with his old general, into the vortex of the Revolution, had afterwards retired to the United States, where like the wise man in the story, he listened to the distant echo of the storm.

Of the unlucky M. de la Fayette we both spoke in a befitting manner; he, because he had always followed him; I, out of gratitude for past favours, and we often also spoke of his share in the American War, in which we had both been actors, and both under his orders. In the course of conversation, M. de la Colombe related to me the history of one of the adventures of our general—a story which my departure for America on my third visit, had prevented my ever hearing before.

"You have heard," he said to me, "how M. de la Fayette quitted, in 1792, the army which he commanded, and came to Paris, and how, after having failed to carry out his good intentions, he returned to Maubeuge, with the sad conviction that he would not be able to do any good, or prevent any evil, either in Paris, or with the army. You know that finding himself in this difficulty he deserted his party, and, with some of his officers, presented himself at the Austrian advanced post, and demanded permission to pass. This permission might easily have been refused, but there was no justification for arresting the party, for, as you are of course aware, all that they wished to do was to get to Ostend and then come over here. To the shame and disgrace of the Prince of Cobourg, however, or rather to the Court of Vienna, M. de la Fayette and the officers who accompanied him, were all made prisoners and closely confined in the citadel of Olmutz. You know that I was one of his companions in misfortune, but you do not know, for it is not known in Europe, of the plan, its preparations, and the carrying out of his escape, which only failed through his own fault, for he *did* escape, and was, so to speak, wrecked in port. Here is the story.

"General Washington, who was still President at that time, made instant applications to the Cabinet of Vienna to obtain his friend's liberty, but met with a formal refusal. A plan of escape was then arranged over here, and Congress devoted a sum of 400,000 francs to its execution. You have seen almost every day, at Philadelphia, the man who was charged to carry out the scheme; it was a German doctor, named Bollman, a man of ability, who did not need to be taught his lesson. Time was needed to carry out the scheme, and a good deal of audacity had to be concealed under a good deal of skill and prudence.

"Having provided himself with excellent letters of recommendation the doctor arrived at Hamburg, as though to exercise his profession in Germany. He lived in good style, kept a carriage, visited the sick poor without a fee, and did many charitable acts in a simple and unaffected manner, though he followed in the footsteps of Cagliostro and the

famous Count St. Germain. He was as slow as a
tortoise in accomplishing his end; stopped in all
the principal towns of Germany, and when after a very
slow progress, he did arrive at Olmutz, he had
already achieved a reputation for science, kindness,
and philanthropy. He did not omit to pay a visit
to the governor of the fortress as soon as he arrived, and quickly made the acquaintance of that
worthy German, who often came to see him, and
invited him to dinner. The champagne was not
spared on these occasions, and, at length, one day,
over the bottle, the doctor hinted that he had heard
in the town that a prisoner of some importance,
who was under the governor's care, was in a precarious state of health. He remarked that, in his
own interest, the governor should see to this, as if
the prisoner died, his death would be imputed to
neglect or ill-treatment, and the odium of that charge
would rest not only on the gaoler, but even on the
sovereign.

"The guileless governor grew fearful of the consequences that might ensue, and begged the doctor's help and advice, and the other protested that
as a good and loyal German he was ready to do
everything he could for the patient. Trusting in
the good faith of Dr. Bollman, the governor conducted him into the prisoner's cell. The doctor
took advantage of the opportunity, and whilst feeling
M. de la Fayette's pulse, slipped into his hand a
note which informed him of the plot, and raised his

hopes of ultimate escape. Bollman gravely informed the governor that the prisoner would inevitably die in a brief space of time if he were not allowed to breathe the fresh air of the country. Owing to the feeble condition of the invalid no fear of his escape need be entertained, and the doctor concluded by saying that he would take the prisoner for occasional drives in his own carriage, which should only proceed at a walking pace, and could be escorted by any soldiers the governor thought necessary. That functionary,—never suspecting a doctor who had such good wine,—gave his consent.

"M. de la Fayette, for his part, pretended to be extremely weak, and even unable to walk, so he was carried to the carriage, which never took him more than a league from Olmutz, and always brought him to the appointed spot when the drive was finished. This went on for some time, and the governor feeling more secure, gradually diminished the escort, and finally reduced it to a single soldier.

"Meanwhile the cunning physician bought two fine saddle horses, and arranged to have them taken to a certain spot at a certain hour on an appointed day. Bollman also provided a couple of pairs of pistols, and plenty of money. When they arrived at the place arranged, they jumped out of the carriage, and the doctor with one hand presented a pistol at the head of the astonished soldier, and with the other offered him a purse of gold. Then the horses appeared, and the two fugitives sprang to the saddle and rode off. After going some distance they separated. M. de la Fayette rode fifty miles on the same horse which at last dropped dead, and he was imprudent enough to stop to buy another. In Germany it is the custom to fire a cannon when a prisoner has escaped, and the peasants, being therefore on the look-out for any suspected person, arrested M. de la Fayette for the sake of the reward they would get for his capture, and took him back to Olmutz. The doctor who acted more circumspectly, got away, and returned to America alone."

Such was the story told by my friend La Colombe. When I afterwards returned to Paris, I met M. de la Fayette, who said to me with a laugh:

"Well! I also have been in a fortress, and tried to make my escape."

"So I hear," I replied, "but you did not manage it as well as I did, General."

Shortly afterwards I left the United States,—this time "for good" I think,—and landed at Hamburg.

CHAPTER VII

Arrival at Hamburg—Departure for France—I become a smuggler at Antwerp—Condition of France—My residence in France—Departure for Trieste—Joseph la Brosse, the banker—The Governors, Junot, Bertrand, Fouché (Duke of Otrante), Gustavson, King of Sweden—Jérôme Bonaparte.

I BELIEVE I am not exaggerating when I say that this city, and Altona, which is only separated from it by a fine avenue of trees, then contained seven or eight thousand French *émigrés*.

Hamburg, being a neutral city, did an immense business, and offered even more opportunity than the United States for the industry and activity of our French *émigrés*, who were obliged to make a living somehow. Some wrote books, and others sold them.

I met there a M. de P——, who had a small capital of a hundred louis. He exchanged money, and was obliged to trot about the town like a messenger, exchanging ducats, piastres, sequins, and crowns, according to the requirements of the persons he met, but he managed to make his ten francs every day.

I also found there a young Frenchman, who did

not know mathematics, but managed to teach the Germans all the same. As he spoke the language well he went every morning to a friend, a German naval officer, to take a lesson, and then carried his newly acquired information to his pupils, who each paid him a mark. If a pupil made any observation, the professor refused to give an explanation, in order, as he said, not to confuse the pupil's mind. When his lesson was finished he received his money, out of which he had to give ten cents to the naval officer.

In fact the *émigrés* busied themselves to such an extent in every department of commerce, that the Jews seemed likely at one time to leave the field to them. One Jew who was a painter, revenged himself by taking a likeness on the quiet of the Frenchman he most disliked,—a certain R—— F——, I believe. He represented him as sitting in one pan of a pair of scales, whilst in the other were twenty Jews who were unable to weigh him up. The caricature was sold in the print shops.

I had left my brother and his family established at Lausanne, where they had founded a house of business which promised to extend and prosper. I learned in a singular manner that his success had surpassed all his hopes. At Hamburg I heard some talk of a banker, a second " philosopher without knowing it," another M. Vanderk in fact, who under the name of Joseph la Brosse, had established a solid and flourishing business at Trieste. A draft of 100,000 florins drawn on him was paid at sight.

I soon found out that this millionaire was no other than my brother. The invasion of Switzerland by the French had caused him to quit Lausanne, and he had carried his Lares and Penates to Trieste. For some years past he had made that city the head-quarters of his business, and his commercial transactions had increased to an enormous extent. I formed a project to go and visit my brother, but I did not carry it into effect for some time, for chance threw in my way an opportunity of visiting Paris.

The circumstances under which this opportunity arrived were amusing, and I might say instructive. I have no compunction in mentioning them, for it is not probable that there will ever be another emigration from France, and, if there should be, it would be the citizens who had nothing who would rob the citizens who had property—that is the invariable rule. We of the old nobility would not be the sufferers, for, heaven knows, few indeed of the fine castles, mansions, and fortunes, have remained in the families of their original owners.

But, at any rate if the so-called liberalism—which is very different from the old Jacobinism, because it has the red cap in its pocket instead of on its head—if liberalism, I say, should ever drive the wealth out of France, I thought I should like to know how it came back.

I did not look forward with much pleasure to my visit to France, and had no family ties, for my relations had either been murdered or driven out of the country, but there was danger to be incurred by returning.

Nitimur in vetitum semper cupimusque negata.

I meant to preserve my incognito, and hoped that my friends,—if I should meet any,—would also keep it. This mystery, with a spice of danger added, gave promise that my days would not be dull, and besides I wanted to see France from behind the scenes;—to view the carnival in action. The Directoire was still at the Luxembourg, and on the walls, the coins, and at the head of decrees, you read the words, *République Française*, and saw the fasces and the cap of liberty. I had heard all this, but I only half believed it, and, at all events, the spectacle seemed worth witnessing, even at some risk.

To revisit France, if a chance occurred, was a fixed resolve with me, and the chance did occur. One morning while I was at Hamburg, I received a letter, addressed to me, coming from one of the departments annexed to France, and containing an official intimation that the name of my friend, the Chevalier de la Colombe, had been struck off the list of proscribed emigrants. I turned the letter over and over, and said to myself, "Why, this is a permission to bearer. My friend La Colombe cannot fail sooner or later, to hear in the United States, through the newspapers, of the removal of his name. I will ask the French authorities at Altona for a passport in his name for Paris, and it is sure not to be refused."

I presented myself before M. Diétrick, the Resident of the Republic, "one and indivisible." At the moment I arrived a Gascon soldier of the bodyguard was applying for a passport, and was passing himself off for a Swiss. The worthy fellow had nothing against him but his accent.

"Yes, *monsou* le Resident," said the applicant from the South, "I require a passport for France."

"And so you are a Swiss?" said the Resident.

"A Swiss of Neuchatel, *monsou* le Resident," replied the Gascon.

"Monsou le Resident" could not refrain from saying, with a quiet smile, "Since when was Neuchatel situated on the Garonne?"

The imperturbable Gascon was not taken aback, and without moving a muscle, replied, "Ever since the Revolution, *monsou* le Resident."

The retort was unanswerable, and the passport was issued. In my case, the application seemed only a natural consequence of the official document of which I was the bearer, and I obtained the passport without any difficulty. I had borrowed my friend's name, certainly, but the description in the passport referred to me, and I set out on my journey in perfect security.

When I was about to leave, I reviewed the state of my finances, and as I know that what does not increase diminishes. I exchanged a fair number of ducats for English merchandise, which promised me a good profit if I could only succeed in introducing it into French territory,—but how that was to be done I had not calculated, and trusted to luck to help me at the critical moment; *audentes fortuna juvat.*

I arrived at the gates of Antwerp. I had with me in my carriage, perhaps I should say in our carriage, for it belonged to him as much as to me,—or rather it belonged to neither of us, for it was a hired conveyance,—I had with me as my travelling companion, an *émigré* whose name had also been removed from the list of proscriptions. He also was returning to France, but his papers were all in order. M. de P—— was a good, careful, prudent man, much esteemed by all who knew him, and by all who knew his daughter, for he was the father of the good and beautiful Madame de M—— who has the secret of preserving her beauty, for on my word as a man of honour, and a good judge, though she was beautiful at twenty, she was yet more beautiful twenty years later. I acted as escort and protector to my companion, and would not have suffered a hair on his head to be touched, and he had plenty of hairs on his head, for though he was middle-aged he was marvellously well preserved,—it runs in the family.

M. de P—— had nothing to fear, but I was not at all easy in my mind when we drove up to the gates of Antwerp. My merchandise, my papers, my name, my person, were all contraband. The carriage stopped before the lodge of the customs officer, the door was opened, and an officer put his head in and asked the usual question. It was evening, and he carried a lighted candle in his hand. I seized my companion's arm and whispered to him, "Leave everything to me; don't speak, and above all don't laugh." Then having, on the spur of the moment, devised the little comedy I was about to play, I began my part.

"Ah, my dear Durand, how are you?" I cried, stretching forth my hand in the most friendly manner to the customs officer,—whom I had never seen before. "So they have sent you here now."

The man replied, as I had fully expected he would, "Citizen, I don't know you."

With that I jumped out of the carriage, and threw my arms round the neck of my newly-found friend; the candle fell, the customs officer swore and pushed me away, and the inspector came out and asked what was the matter.

"Lieutenant," I said, "I appeal to you. Here is Durand, my old comrade, who won't recognize his friend Bernard, though he taught me the profession."

The inspector listened to what I had to say, the other officers turned out of the guard-house with torches, and the misunderstanding was cleared up, —much to my advantage. The inspector,—to whom I had been careful to apply the title of lieutenant, though he was only a brigadier,—was already disposed in my favour.

That I had been misled by a chance resemblance, and that the customs officer was not my old friend Durand, I was the first to acknowledge, but the inspector and all his assistants,—even the one I had baptized Durand,—were all very polite to me, and attributed the mistake partly to absence of mind, partly to good fellowship. Conversation became general, everyone had something to say;—there were so many posts along the immense frontier, and such transfers and removals almost every day,—and the new post was always so far from the old one,—and a man never knew what it was to have a home,—and, we all agreed, the Revenue Department was very badly managed.

"And now, citizens," I said at last, in the gravest possible manner, "duty must be done, and it is not a customs officer who will refuse to obey the laws of the Republic. Lieutenant, will you please search my trunk? Here is the key."

The "lieutenant" smiled, the others all cried in chorus, "What! search a comrade's box!" I took my leave of them all, put the key back in my pocket, and got into the carriage again. All wished me a good journey and a short stay in my new quarters, for I fancy, that in order to make them pity me the more, I had mentioned Soubise or Marennes as my destination.

Good M. de P—— who had remained in the carriage, still trembled for me. When we had passed the barrier, I laughed and said, "That is the way to smuggle. I could not get out of it as Marshal Saxe did, but you will agree that I managed it pretty well." And thereupon I told him the story of what happened to the conqueror of Fontenoy at the gates of some Flemish town.

Marshal Saxe was returning into France after the campaign of 1745. At the gates of some city on the French frontier, a customs officer presented himself at the door of the carriage, and said, "Have you anything contrary to the orders of the king, Marshal?"

"No, Monsieur."

"But what is that?" asked the officer, pointing to an immense barrel of tobacco on which the marshal's feet were resting, and which took up all the front part of the carriage.

"That, Monsieur," replied the marshal calmly, "is my tobacco box."

"Oh, indeed!" said the official. "Well, I suppose it is but right that a very great general should have a tobacco box in proportion," and he closed the door respectfully.

Success begets confidence, and confidence begets fresh successes, and thus one arrives at high position, fortune, and honours,—but I only wanted to arrive at Paris. There was, however, one more formality to fulfil,—the passport issued at Hamburg, must be *visé* by the authorities of Antwerp. For some months past the chief official there had been called a Prefect,—the post had been newly created by the ruler, who, under the title of First Consul, was sole master in France, though there were professedly three persons at the head of the so-called Republic. France was still nominally a Republic, and individuals who ere long would be called Sire, Monseigneur, Duke, Baron, or Excellency, were still simple citizens.

I went to the Prefecture of Antwerp, and presented myself before the chief magistrate of the department. I was announced as M. de la Colombe.

"Yes, Citizen Prefect, I am M. de la Colombe, an *émigré rayé*, from Hamburg, and I want my passport *visé* in order to return to France."

"*M. de la Colombe*," said the prefect, in a marked manner, that I ought to have noticed, and looking at me in a droll sort of way. "Please to take a chair, *M. de la Colombe*. Have I the honour of addressing *M. de la Colombe?* It is not long since *M. de la Colombe* left Hamburg. You only received the intimation of the removal of your name from the list a few days ago, I suppose, *M. de la Colombe*. We are delighted, *M. de la Colombe*, to be able to provide French *émigrés* with the means of returning to their mother country. *M. de la Colombe* wants his passport *visé* for Paris. I hope *M. de la Colombe* will not meet with any unpleasantness during his stay in the capital. I am glad to have had the honour of making your acquaintance, *M. de la Colombe*. I have the honour to wish you a pleasant and prosperous journey, *M. de la Colombe*."

It was "*M. de la Colombe*" all the time. "The prefect is extremely polite," I said to myself, "but is he afraid that people will forget their own names?" Some time afterwards, however, I learned that the Prefect of Antwerp was the stranger who had forwarded to me at Hamburg,—through a third person,—the notice of the removal of the name of La Colombe,—with whom he had formerly been very intimate. Then I had the key to the enigma, and understood his kindness, discretion, and genial banter, for instead of signing the *visa* to my passport, he could have told me openly that I was an impostor, and I should have had no right to complain.

I ought to mention, as a matter of historical accuracy, that I am not quite sure, at this length of time, whether it was the prefect or the secretary-general with whom I had to do, but at this period there were many instances besides mine, in which functionaries did all they could to modify the rigours of the Osselin law. A certain great personage, whom I will not name, may perhaps remember this incident, which is greatly to his honour. An *émigré* applied to him, in the name of Bouchard. "I can do nothing for Citizen Bouchard," was the reply, "but I will do all in my power for M. de Montmorenci."

Anyhow, there I was in France, and when I arrived in Paris, I was as much under the shelter of the law as any inhabitant who had never quitted the country, or meddled in political events.

"His native land is dear to each true heart!
With what delight do I behold this spot."

That is what nearly everyone feels, and nearly everyone says,— from Tancred to Potaveri, from the Frenchman to the Hottentot;—but I said nothing of the kind.

The ruling inclination in me,—it has been a slight fault of mine ever since I was twenty years of age, —is to indulge in a private chuckle, and so I admire very little, and I rarely blame, and though I do not laugh outright, I laugh in my beard, for I have seen so much that I have learned to estimate events at their proper value, and I praise no celebrity till after he is dead;—I have made so many mistakes in paying my tribute of admiration to a living celebrity. This disposition made me regard France as a very absurd set of magic lantern slides. When I had been forty-eight hours in Paris, it seemed to me that of all the persons I recognized, the pretty women had grown old, and the men had changed.

I had always prided myself on the possession of a well-shaped leg, and had always been in favour of knee breeches and stockings, and when I saw everyone wearing trousers, I said to myself, " Has the Revolution made all the young men bow-legged?" Similarly when I saw double or single eye-glasses on the noses of young men of twenty, I said, " This unlucky Revolution has made them all short-sighted." I know that, as a general rule, the public cannot see beyond its nose, but when I noticed that it was merely a freak of fashion and that the young men got themselves up as carefully as Antinous, I thought perhaps they wore eye-glasses in order to better resemble the favourite of Adrian, and I laughed at those historians who pretend that glasses are a modern invention.

I saw pass along the Boulevards two young men, dressed in the very height of fashion, mounted on fine horses, and trotting at a rate which made every-one turn to look at them. A middle-aged man, who was leaning on his cane, watching them, cried as they passed him,—in the tone which an uncle or a father would have used—"Very pretty indeed,—but the debts!" They both laughed, and so did I. I knew them, and the reproof was not undeserved, as regards one of them at least.

Another time I saw in a fine carriage,—and there were not many such at Paris at that time,—a face that I recognized by its ineptitude. He was a *virtuoso* whom I remembered as making his *début* at a concert, and with the greatest possible success, when he was a beardless boy. I had not forgotten that he said to me, as we came out, "Did I not play like an angel?" I must confess that he must have had some talent in his fingers, for this young fool became a millionaire in six months, and has managed to keep his money; so if he was a fool he was no ass,—but it is not worth while to mention his name.

As for me, I had at once, as a precautionary measure, taken up my residence in the quietest quarter of the city I could find, that is to say in the Rue St. Louis in the Marais. I had not been a week in Paris,— trying the ground to make sure it was safe, when I unexpectedly encountered an old acquaintance. The meeting made me uneasy at first, but in the end was most fortunate and useful for me. I remember (though now with pleasure and gratitude) that my first feeling at this encounter was one of fear. It was exactly like the meeting between Almaviva and the Barber of Seville. The good fellow,—whom I took for something quite different,—scanned me so closely, that I said to myself, "I have seen him somewhere."

"I am not mistaken," he said, "it is you, M. le Chevalier."

"Ah, it is you, d'O——," I answered with a little more confidence, "and what are you doing at Paris." When I left in '91 he was proprietor of a café at the Petit Carreau.

D'O—— had been brought up by my grandmother and my uncle, the President. He was a tall, good-looking man, with a frank open face, and, when I knew him, very active, strong, and exceedingly bold, though he carried no weapons, offensive or defensive, except a little stick about a foot and a half long, and no thicker than a switch. He looked a little older, but otherwise was externally very much as I had known him. However, I guessed from his character, that he was not likely to have remained neutral during the Revolutionary troubles, and I was doubtful of what he might have become during the ten years which had elapsed since I had lost sight of him. All the difference between us and the characters in Beaumarchais' play was, that I was not a grandee of Spain, that we were on the pavement of Paris, and that honest d'O—— was, has always been, and is still, the best and worthiest of men;—otherwise his story greatly resembled that of Figaro.

"Yes," he said to me, "I was, when you left France, proprietor of a café. I became what is called *officier de paix*, and had to guard the Tuileries. You may guess that I showed our unfortunate king and his august family every mark of devotion, and there was no advice likely to be useful for their safety or repose that I failed to give them. They did me the honour to receive me, and confide in me as a servant in whom they could trust. After the terrible day of the 10th of August, I was arrested, and brought to trial. I pleaded my own cause, I defended my head with courage and eloquence, and *as I had the advantage* of not being noble, but belonging to the people, they were forced to forgive me for having done my duty, and I was acquitted. I wore the livery of the Revolution, but nevertheless I carried in my heart a love of the Bourbons, and of all honest people. I have saved as many as I could from the scaffold; many know it, but many others do not suspect it, for I never told them, fearing lest their indiscreet gratitude might compromise me and prevent me fror serving others. I was adroit, and feared nothing, though I rarely carried any weapon except the little 'Jacob's staff' you see here—sometimes I had a pair of pistols in my pockets, but I never had occasion to use them; and I was so honest that they gave me *carte blanche* for my expenses and paid my accounts without examining them.

"The Committee of Public Safety often sent me on missions, with powers exceeding even those of the Representatives of the people themselves, and thus I was able to do good service by making away with documents which would have destroyed whole families. I often took away papers, when I was sure that the Committee knew nothing of the affairs to which they related, and it was in this way that I saved the lives of the Comte and Comtesse de T—— who are related to your family. Ah, why was I not able to save your unfortunate uncle? but I did not know what danger he was in, and the scoundrels were too quick for me.

"At last I was put in prison myself, but I got out again, and was put in again,—according as the factions which were disputing for power gained or lost,—every three months; and then the 9th Thermidor arrived. The accomplices of Robespierre themselves felt that divine vengeance of which they had been the instruments. Thus, sometimes in favour, and sometimes in prison, but superior to fortune in either case, praised by some, blamed by others, taking advantage of fair weather, and caring little for the bad, and thwarting the wicked, I, with all my boldness and activity have come at last to be commissary of police in a quarter where everybody goes to bed at nine o'clock,—and am ready to serve you in any way that you may be pleased to command.

"Finally I was transported, but in very good company. It was a trick of Fouché, who wanted to be even with me, and I could do nothing. I made the voyage with Pichegru, and a lot of others, but they were all bewildered and lost their heads, for what use are great statesmen, famous warriors, and distinguished personages when you remove them from their familiar surroundings.

"It was I who found the boat and prepared the flight; and brought six besides myself safe and sound to Surinam. I remembered you, Chevalier, and do you know that it is no easier to get away from Cayenne than it is from Pierre-en-Cize; there are difficulties in both cases. At any rate I came back from Cayenne, and though I have been buffeted about by adversity, the wind is in my favour now, and 'I am ready to serve you in any way you may please to command', as the hero of Beaumarchais' play says,—though, by the way, he had not been through so much as I have. I am as well known as Barabbas, and I know everybody, good or bad. Speak, you have but to command."

The meeting, though absurd, was very useful for me. Through my friend d'O———, I discovered that I was not on the list of *émigrés*. There had been some intention of putting my name down, but they had not my Christian names properly, one of them had been forgotten, and my identity was not exact. Such was the ridiculous state of the law at that time,—a letter killed or saved a man,—but when they did have your name properly you were put down as a supposed *émigré*, even if you had been in prison all the time since 1792.

When I found that I was not on the list, I was not satisfied with my good luck, and was bold enough to demand an account of property. But my case remained unsettled, perhaps because I had selected for my attorney, Jacques Déloges. I passed the 3rd Nivôse quietly enough, I only heard the report of the explosion in the Rue Saint Nicaise, and I was not in the secret. My friend d'O — assured me that Fouché would visit on the red caps all the wrath of Jupiter, the First Consul. But I saw taken to the Temple only a few days later, some persons who were certainly not "reds" but "whites", and I came to the conclusion that the air of Paris was not good for me, and I might find a purer and better atmosphere. I was taken with the reverse of homesickness, and felt as much desire to get out of the country as I had formerly done to get into it.

I knew very well that, unless I went to England, I should, out of France, be still under the same rule, visible or invisible, but the Temple, Vincennes, and the plain of Grenelle, robbed Paris of all its charms. The occupant of the Tuileries had sworn that the sun should not set on his dominions, and that he would everywhere do as he liked, but it struck me that the rays of his sun would not burn me so much if I were at a distance.

I said to myself, "*Italiam! Italiam!*" for I remembered that on the Adriatic Sea I had a second home, where I should meet a fraternal welcome, for my elder brother, the head of the family, had there gathered together the household gods.

D'O—— had procured for me, in case of accidents, passports made out in a false name, but with my correct description, and it was well for me that I used them at the right moment. The day of my departure, poor d'O——, my political barometer, received, as a kind attention from Fouché, an "invitation" to retire to M—— and remain there until further orders. That only made me set off the faster towards Trieste, and as straight as I could go. I never looked behind me till I had passed the frontier of my native land, where, under the rule of the benign Bonaparte, no one was ever sure of sleeping in his bed at night.

The word "prison" had always made me prick up my ears like a hare, and I was singularly well-instructed in the topography of France, as regards the dungeons. I wished that the angels could have carried the diligence, as they did the house of the Virgin from Capernaum to Loretto, for I felt quite a nightmare when I saw on my left the castle of Joux, where M. de Suzannet then was, and, as we skirted the Doubs, the citadel of Besançon above my head to the left. I breathed more freely when, entering Lyon by the faubourg of Vaise, I noticed that Pierre-en-Cize was pulled down, and nobody else could be put there,—at least until it was rebuilt,— and I said to myself, "Well, it is certain that poor M. de L——, who wanted so much to escape, is no longer there."

And so with my heart full of kindly thoughts, I passed,—either that day or the next,—the bridge of Beauvoisin, and so from town to town, traversed the Kingdom of Italy, and the former Republic of Venice, where I did not see the Lion of St. Mark, because I had left it at Paris in front of the Invalides. I did not seek the *Bucentaur*, but a little felucca, and with my usual good luck, found one all ready to sail for Trieste. The felucca received me and my baggage, and the sea which the Doge of Venice weds every year, did not seem to notice the light weight I laid on its back, and in due time I landed safely at that city which for some time past had been known as the capital of the Illyrian provinces, and,—speaking without prejudice,—I found the air there better.

I saw at once that I was not mistaken in supposing that I should be safe there. The country had been but recently annexed, and the people had just submitted themselves. The two-legged mules still carried their burden, though the pack was marked with another letter, and it was politic not to make the new load heavier than the old one. Trieste was the most advanced outpost of the French Republic, and it was difficult to believe it would be held for a long term. The adventurer who governed France spent his years in playing at war, and risked all for all in each battle.

Placed thus at the top of the gulf, I had in front of me the Adriatic Sea, which stretched like a long street between the former Republic of Venice, the former Papal States, and the former Kingdom of the Two Sicilies,—for the time being. Behind me on the north I had the land of the Pandours of Trenk, the Croats of the celebrated Count Serin, of the fortress of Zigeth, semi-savages, whose only claim to civilisation was their fidelity to the Romische Kaiser, and the paternal house of Austria. Peace between such neighbours only depended on circumstances.

On the left, in Epirus and Albania, and as far as Ragusa, little trust could be placed in the natives, and behind these strange French citizens were the Pachas of Trawnik, Nicopolis, Widin, and Janina, who are accustomed to keep all their goods, from their cloaks to their money, in cypress wood coffers, which are *not* fastened to the wall. An uncertainty as to what to-morrow may bring forth is a natural condition of the lives of these Turkish potentates, who sat day after day smoking their pipes at no great distance from us. They afforded me a subject for comparison with the precarious condition of the French in the land to which I had come to seek a stone whereon to rest my head.

The flag of France was flying everywhere, and I saw the tricolour of the Republic, One and Indivisible, instead of the yellow and black flag with the Austrian Eagle, but the occupation was very recent, and our power seemed to me like a house of cards, liable to be blown down by the first ill wind,—though whether it would blow from the north or the south, I could not guess.

Trieste, which is situated at the end of the gulf which bears its name, is built in the form of an amphitheatre on the side of a hill, the foot of which is washed by the sea. A citadel has been constructed on the summit of this hill, and, from its position, commands all the city, which is divided into an upper and a lower town. My brother's house was in the lower part of Trieste, near the port. The Empress Maria Theresa transformed Trieste, which before that was merely a harbour, into a commercial city, the chief, in fact the only, maritime establishment of the Austrian Empire.

From 1750, Trieste had been increasing in size and wealth. In 1767, an Insurance Company, with a capital of 300,000 florins was founded there; and in 1770 it contained thirty large houses of business. At the period of which I am writing, Trieste had arrived at its highest degree of prosperity.

The business which my brother had founded, and which he conducted so honourably and with such success, was now one of the first firms in

Europe. He had gathered round him many of the *émigrés*, former fellow officers of the Dauphiné regiment, and had made them associates with him in his business.

I arrived in time to witness an incident which proved in what consideration my brother was held, on account of his upright conduct.

But a short time before, a French army had presented itself before Trieste, and the city, being incapable of any resistance, surrendered.

The general laid a heavy tax upon the city, and a great part of this fell upon the merchants. They prepared to pay it, and Joseph la Brosse put his own name down at the head of the list for a large amount. But the conquerors had heard that he was a French *émigré*, and knew how he had regained his fortune and the noble use that he made of it, and the French general, being willing to oblige a compatriot who had so bravely struggled against adversity, declared Joseph la Brosse should be exempt from the tax, and pay nothing. My brother asked if his share was to be deducted from the total, and received the reply that though he was personally exempted from paying, no diminution would be made in the sum demanded, but his share would have to be contributed by the other merchants of Trieste. My brother was noble and disinterested enough to reply that he had received the hospitality of Trieste, and all the merchants of the city were his comrades and friends, and that as he had shared with them in good luck, it was only fair that he should be allied with them in their misfortune.

"But," he said to General S——, "as you wish to show me a kindness, there is something you can do for me. Diminish the number of soldiers who are lodged in my warehouses, for I have noticed that bales of merchandise do not seem to agree with sabres and moustaches."

The general laughed, and removed many of the soldiers who were billeted on my brother.

He easily recouped himself, however, for his share in the contribution levied on Trieste, for he made a contract with the general for supplying the army with all that it needed, charging only a small commission. The contract was duly carried out to the satisfaction of both parties.

My brother had a town house in Trieste, where he carried on his business as a banker, and merchant, and he had also a country house, or as it might more properly be called, an estate, with a handsome residence to match. His time was thus always occupied either by agriculture or commerce, and each hour of the day had its useful and praiseworthy employment. The management of the internal arrangements belonged to my sister-in-law, but she had a hand in foreign affairs also, managed the correspondence in the absence of her husband, and often gave sound advice on business affairs connected with the firm of Joseph la Brosse & Co.

The Continental blockade greatly assisted my brother's speculations. The Levant cottons could no longer come by sea, and had to be brought overland, and he had much to do with the transport, and brought a great part of the best cotton into Europe. He thus became acquainted with some of the chief bankers of Paris. In connection with this I will relate an anecdote showing a comic contrast between two different kinds of men.

I was along with my brother in Paris, whither he had returned to see if the waters of the political deluge had really retired from France, and if he could take back, like the dove, a green leaf to his family, who had remained in the ark of safety at Trieste.

A *confrère*, one of the leading commercial men in Paris, and between whom and my brother there existed a mutual esteem and friendship, came to congratulate him on his arrival. He had exalted notions of the dignity of commerce, and in the course of conversation, he said,

"You must own, Monsieur, that you have led quite a different life since you took to business. Now, your signature is worth a hundred thousand crowns, from one end of Europe to the other, and you are known everywhere as Joseph la Brosse. Is not that better than being called the Comte de Pontgibaud? At the best you would have been no better off than a couple of thousand others, whilst to-day——"

The door opened and the Archbishop of Rouen entered. He embraced my brother, and said,

"So, my dear Pontgibaud, you have at last come back to us. Well, of course, you will stop with us. Leave behind your counter, and your borrowed name of Joseph la Brosse, and again resume your place as our old friend, Comte de Pontgibaud."

You may guess how laughable this contrast sounded, especially to my brother, who did not say a word. It is nevertheless true, that at the time of the Continental blockade, my brother, who was previously a millionaire, possessed a fortune much greater than he had possessed, or ever could have possessed, in France. He was a merchant, banker, and landed proprietor, for he had, near Trieste, a fine house with plenty of land. The astute merchant of the city was, in the country, an able agriculturist, for throughout his life he had a taste for farming. He combined theory with practice, and did not, like "parlour farmers," content himself with inventing useless systems, but tried experiments which nearly always succeeded.

Being of an observant turn of mind, he found something to do at all hours and in all weathers, when he was on his estate. If rain fell in torrents we would all make for the house, but he would go out again in the heaviest shower to study the direction that the water took in different places, and utilize his knowledge in irrigating, or draining, his land. Fortune was bound to come to one who sought her by all roads.

His relations with all sorts of people, as a commercial notability, and more recently as a banker, had rendered his name known throughout Europe. As for me, I had sunk from an actor to become a spectator. My dear brother, the most sensible, calmest, and most virtuous of men, would have been glad to do for me what he had done for many others, if I had been obliged to have recourse to him. His genius,—for so I might call it,—could not be compared to his character, which was one of the most noble I have ever known. In short, his wisdom and intelligence were only equalled by his kindness, his probity, his humanity, and complaisance, and it might be well said of him,

"*Homo sum, humani nihil à me alienum puto.*"

But it is true that the services he rendered other people often turned to his own profit, without any intention on his part. Accidents even conspired to increase not only his fortune and reputation, but the esteem, good will, and gratitude which all felt towards him. The justice that was done to his character, the confidence that was shown in him, the protection and shelter that many came to ask of him, are satisfactory proofs that the human species does not wholly consist of wolves and sheep, torturers and their victims, tyrants and oppressed; an example to the contrary was to be found every day at Trieste, where I have often watched with my own eyes, as in a magic lantern, all the most dramatic personages of Continental Europe pass one after the other.

Trieste became a refuge where all the political cripples, of whatever rank they were, discrowned kings and their ministers, came to seek asylum, and found it; my brother received them all under his hospitable roof.

For several years there was an almost daily succession of celebrated refugees, of all sorts and conditions. My brother was all things to all men, and was generally looked upon as the friend of humanity. He resembled Captain Cook, who sailed between two hostile fleets of savages, who were preparing to attack each other, and was saluted by both sides. His conduct at Trieste reminded me of that rich and pious citizen of Agrigentum who, it was said, sat at the gates of the city of Agrigentum in order to be the first to offer hospitality to the travellers who arrived. He imitated Gellias without knowing it, and his kindness and delicacy were so much appreciated that all strangers of distinction were either sent or came to him. In fact, Joseph la Brosse of Trieste exactly resembled the colossal figure of St. Christopher, which is put at the door of some churches in order that it may be seen afar off, and in accordance with the popular belief expressed in the monkish Latin proverb, *Christophorum videas postea tutus eas*. But it is doubtful whether even the great St. Christopher did as much good as my brother was able to do.

Not long after my arrival, General Junot was named " Captain General and Governor of the Illyrian Provinces." He had great confidence in my brother, and treated him with consideration and regard, but the sun of Portugal had had a bad effect on the head of this *sabreur*, who naturally was neither sober nor prudent. Though he held a relatively high position in the Empire, General Junot compromised his prospects by giving daily examples of extravagant and absurd conduct. One day when reviewing the troops, he drove in front of the soldiers in a carriage with four horses, and as he passed along he struck the men with his whip, crying at the same time, "Fall in line! Fall in line!" He committed many other absurdities, and at last orders arrived at Trieste from the Viceroy that he was to be seized and sent back to Paris. The instructions were bound to be obeyed, but the task was not an easy one. Finally a corn sack was thrown over his head, and he was tied up like a bale of tobacco, put in his own carriage, and packed off to Paris.

At his departure, his tradespeople and other creditors surrounded his house, and refused to allow his baggage to be removed till their claims were satisfied. My brother, seeing a large crowd at the door squabbling over the cases and trunks, inquired the cause of the disturbance. He was told that the general's property was detained for debts amounting to two thousand crowns. My brother paid all claims upon the spot, without waiting for any instructions, and released the goods, which duly arrived safely in Paris. The cases contained much valuable property, and the diamond stars and orders which had been presented to the general. The Duchesse d'Abrantes wrote a letter of thanks to my brother, and added that her first care should be to repay the debt. In fact, as soon as her husband's affairs were settled, a draft for 2000 crowns was sent to Trieste, in repayment of the sum which had been so obligingly advanced.

General Bertrand succeeded General Junot as Governor-General of Illyria and the adjacent provinces.* He was honest, just, liberal, and unselfish. He wished to make his new subjects love the rule of his master,—to whom he was himself sincerely attached. He rendered the imperial yoke as light as possible; no small task, as the people could remember still the paternal government of the House of Austria, but at least General Bertrand was both just and generous. In order that his charity might not be imposed on, he charged my brother, who had the reputation of being a strictly honest man, to distribute the money, etc., given to the poor and needy, and to make all inquiries about the applicants for relief, and thus it happened that Joseph la Brosse, a French *émigré*, found himself accidentally acting as an officer of that Emperor of whom his subordinates used to say, " Our master wishes us to shear his sheep, but not flay them."

This noble general, who was called elsewhere,

* This is an error on the part of the author; Bertrand *preceded* Junot. ED

had for a more or less immediate successor a man of quite a different stamp, the celebrated Fouché, Duke of Otranto,—another personage whom Joseph la Brosse saved from misfortune.

Bonaparte lost all the ground he had gained, and as his armies were driven back towards France, all the legations packed their papers into wagons and returned to Paris. The Austrians in their turn took the offensive as the French retired before them. The French still occupied Trieste, though the port was blockaded, and on all the heights which commanded the town were Austrian flags, and batteries of artillery ready to open fire, if any resistance were shown. The notorious Duc d'Otrante, shut up like a wolf in a sheep-fold, was in the greatest trouble.

I was present when he came and begged my brother to save him and his children. Joseph la Brosse was quite a refuge of the wicked, and even Fouché did not have to appeal in vain. He soothed and comforted his visitor, and promised not only to save him but to send after him all his property which he was ready to abandon. The former priest of the Oratory was transformed into a soldier, mounted on a horse amongst fifty gendarmes, and boldly passed through the Austrian lines without being noticed.

Thus was the Duc d'Otrante taken out of danger by Joseph la Brosse, and got away safe and unhurt, and the Dauphin granted a safeguard to one of the worst scoundrels known to history. *

During this political crisis, my brother went from Trieste, which was still occupied by the French, to the Austrian camp, and from the Austrian camp to Trieste, as an emissary in the confidence of both parties. His country house and property were always respected, and regarded indeed as neutral ground.

Fouché had hardly left when Count Gottorp, the ex-king of Sweden, descended, or rather ascended, —for the Prince lived on the second floor,—at the house of Joseph la Brosse.

It could not be said of this monarch at least, that he had no ancestors, and had not been brought up in the Tyrian purple and the royal ermine; he was no Lithuanian gentleman promoted to be King of Poland by the favour of a Muscovite arch-duchess. I had seen, face to face, one kind of sovereign,—a President of the United States,—but it needed another Revolution in another country to bring before my eyes the spectacle of a legitimate " King by the Grace of God" in the house of a simple citizen. Thrones were slippery at the beginning of the Nineteenth Century, and hereditary kings were no better off than those whom chance had presented with a sceptre.

At any rate the royal descendant of Gustavus Adolphus and Charles XII, the son and successor of that Gustavus III who was preparing to lead the

* See Note R.

chivalry of Europe against French Jacobinism at the moment when he was so treacherously murdered by one of his own officers and subjects, was now our guest at Trieste, and living on the second floor in the same house with us. His generals had turned traitors, and dethroned him, and he was now travelling about Europe under the name of Count Gottorp.

He frequently came down to see us and would converse without any ceremony, but he always seemed to me to prefer the company of my brother and my sister-in-law, who never forgot that he had been King of Sweden, though he appeared to forget it himself and to wish that it should be forgotten. My imperturbable sister-in-law, though she joined in the conversation with good-sense and modesty, never neglected, on his account, to see to her household, or the business of the firm. The prince talked freely on all subjects, and showed some learning and a good deal of "superficial knowledge"—but he was a volcano in a state of calm.

His opinions upon different persons were in marked contrast to what,—according to general belief,—they were expected to be. Thus, he said of M. Fersen, "His zeal did me a great deal of harm;" and of the Duke of Sudermania his uncle, who became Charles XIII, "I am under the greatest obligations to him."

Amongst the singularities which rendered his private life so strange, I remarked the following traits.

He always had three courses brought to table for his dinner but he would lock up one of them in his bureau to serve for his supper.

Beggars in Trieste go from house to house and knock at the doors. The king always had a pocketful of money for them, and as soon as he heard a beggar knock he would run downstairs from the second floor to bestow alms upon the mendicant. Indeed he gave very little trouble to the few servants he had, doing much for himself even in his rooms, like Charles XII when he was at Bender.

However, his ideas were, in general, sound and sure enough on all subjects,—with one exception. He had one bugbear; and if, unfortunately, the conversation reminded him of the violence which Generals Klingsporr, Adelscreutz, and his Chamberlain, Silvespare, had shown towards him in his own palace,—or of his imprisonment, with his family, in the fortress of Drottningholm, and the act of abdication which he was forced to sign in June, 1809,—his feelings would carry him away, and his head,—but, stop! it was a crowned head, and, whatever I recollect, I must not forget that.

I remember also that he wished to make a pilgrimage to Jerusalem. When he was on board the ship that he had chartered to convey him to the Holy Land, my brother sent his son,—my nephew, —with some cases of liqueurs, some tea, chocolate, etc., as a farewell gift and token of respect. The prince did the young man the honour to ask him to lunch, but he secretly gave orders to have the anchor weighed, and when the lunch was over, my nephew found that the vessel was sailing along, and that Trieste was out of sight. Finding that the King of Sweden wanted to make him a pilgrim in spite of himself, he protested energetically against the abduction, and with a good deal of trouble obtained permission to be put on shore. His object in carrying off the young man was, apparently, an idea that travel helped greatly to form the mind. Some trivial circumstance, however, brought the prince back again a very short time afterwards. *

It was decreed that all sorts of royalties, the real article and the imitation, should meet at the house of Joseph la Brosse. Whilst the King of Sweden was lodging with us, Jérôme, otherwise known as the King of Westphalia, arrived. I thought that the Carnival of Venice had been transported to Trieste, at the sight of this second King Theodore, more of a Corsican even than his ancestors.

My brother's appearance was so simple, his face was so calm, and his bearing so much in harmony with figures, and book-keeping by double entry, that on seeing him at his desk, you would have sworn that he had been brought up to the business all his life. He was quietly working one morning, when a young man in a frock coat buttoned up to his chin, entered, and asked if that was the house of the

* See Note 8.

banker, Joseph la Brosse. My brother inclined his head slightly, and looked at the stranger with Teutonic unconcern. The young man took out of his pocket-book a draft for a large sum, on the firm of Joseph la Brosse.

My brother quickly noticed that the stranger had a pocketful of these documents, and the unknown, not caring to preserve his incognito any longer, stated that he was the King of Westphalia, and undoing his coat displayed a whole row of orders, the indubitable signs of the forced attentions which all the monarchs of Europe were compelled to pay to all those who bore the name of Bonaparte. Joseph la Brosse did not move a bit faster or slower, and did not say a word the more, in spite of the dazzling display of a complete assortment of stars, eagles, lions, elephants, and what-not, stuck over the pectoral region of the former King Jérôme, but he sent to inform the King of Sweden that His Majesty the King of Westphalia was in the house, asking if he wished to see him.*

"The King of the second story," replied the prince, "is not anxious to meet the King of the ground floor, but the Queen is my cousin, and if she is in Trieste I should be very glad to see her."

After such august personages have figured in my recollections, I do not care to continue any longer.

The year 1814 arrived, when must perish "that man of fate whom God had appointed to punish

* See Note T.

the human race and torture the world. The justice of God had chosen this man to be the minister of its vengeance. He existed to work out the designs of Providence. He thought that he was actuated by his own wishes and passions, and he was really executing the decrees of heaven. Before he fell he had time to ruin peoples and nations, to set fire to the four corners of the earth, to spoil the present and the future by the evils which he did, and by the examples which he left."

How could Balzac, who died in 1655, write that about Cromwell? He certainly foresaw the existence of Napoleon the Great, and,—without excepting Bonaparte himself,—it may be said that he was the only person in France or Europe to show that foresight. But my quotation is only inserted to draw attention to a little-known and singular fact in history, for from the great political giant of the Nineteenth Century I have personally received neither benefit nor injury.

The year 1814 came, and with it the restoration of the legitimate monarchy. I have called this restoration miraculous, and I blessed it with all my heart, with all my soul, and with all my strength,—but, alas, since 1814, I can remember, without any great effort of memory, that I have seen two restorations, and,——but here I will lay down my pen.

THE END.

BIOGRAPHICAL NOTES.

Note A, page 1.

THE opening passage of the book is the only one which it has been found necessary to change. It runs in the original as follows:—

"Je me souviens d'avoir lu qu'en 1637 la reine Anne d'Autriche habitait à Paris: le roi Louis XIII retournant de Vincennes à Saint Germain fut surpris par un violent orage, et coucha aux Tuileries; Louis-le-Grand, naquit le 5 Septembre 1638. En lisant dans l'histoire de France et cette remarque et ce rapprochement, je me suis toujours rappelé, mais jamais sans rire, que feu mon père, qui avait des préventions contre moi, m'a dit plus d'une fois; "Monsieur, vous ne seriez pas là, si telle nuit, telle année, je n'avais pas trouvé des puces dans mon lit." Le lit conjugal fut naturellement et légitimement le refuge de monsieur mon père: je suis devenu, le plus honnêtement du monde, l'éffet de cette cause, et je suis né sous les auspices des puces, le 21 avril 1758, etc."

It may here be remarked that the Chevalier, though he gives the date of his birth correctly, has made a mistake of a year, either in the date of his imprisonment or in the time he was at Pierre-en-Cize. As La Fayette was already in America when Pontgibaud joined him, either the *lettre de cachet* must be postdated by a year or the Chevalier was 30 months, not 18, in prison.

Note B, page 44.

Comte de la Rouarie,—known in the American army as Colonel Armand,—had a strange career. He was born in 1756 at St. Malo, and, when quite a young man, obtained a commission in one of the regiments of Royal body-guards. Though destined afterwards to become one of the staunchest supporters of royalty, he was at first almost a republican, before the Republic was thought of, and his free and fearless criticisms on the Court, caused him to be regarded with disfavour by the military authorities. He did not improve his prospects by falling madly in love with Mlle Beaumesnil,* a pretty, but not very clever actress, who was his uncle's mistress, and proposing to marry her. She refused him, very sensibly remarking that their marriage would create a scandal, involve his social ruin, and ultimately cause him to loathe her. Finding that she was firm in her resolve, he first fought a duel with Comte Bourbon-Brisset,—whom he believed to be a favoured rival,—and then retired to the Monastery of La Trappe.

When the war broke out in America, he threw aside the monk's cowl, and joined La Fayette. At the termination of the campaign, he returned to France, and when the Revolution occurred espoused the royalist cause. For some time he, as leader of the Breton peasants, carried on a not altogether unsuccessful warfare against the Revolutionary troops, but his forces were eventually defeated

* In Michaud's *Biographie Universelle*, the name of the actress is incorrectly given as Mlle Fleury.

or dispersed, and he was forced to disguise himself as a beggar. For eighteen months he wandered about Brittany, and at last, 30th Jan. 1793, died of an illness brought on by exposure, and want of food. His body was buried in a grave dug in the midst of a forest. His "papers" were buried with him, in a glass bottle. One of the Revolutionary spies found out the place of his interment, dug up the grave, and secured the papers. The information thus secured led to the execution of fourteen persons, including the proprietor of the château where La Rouarie had died.

Lebégne Duportail was a very skilful engineer officer. At the end of the American War he returned to France, and was sent to instruct the Neapolitan army in military engineering. A quarrel with one of the Italian Generals led to his early recall. In 1790, La Fayette, who was all-powerful at that time, caused Duportail to be named Minister of War. He imprudently allowed the soldiers to frequent the political clubs. Whilst he was in Lorraine, in 1792, he was "denounced." He at once returned to Paris and remained in concealment for twenty-two months, but in 1794 a law was passed punishing with death all who concealed a proscribed person, and he made his escape to America, and resided there for eight years. In 1802 he was recalled by Bonaparte, but died whilst on the voyage back to France.

Of Duplessis-Mauduit I have been unable to learn any particulars. His name is mentioned in Balch's *Les Français en Amerique*, but, as he died young, and all that he did accomplish was performed in the New World, there is no record of him in French histories.

Note C, page 45.

The "M. Thomas" here alluded to was Antoine Leonard Thomas "of the Academy," born at Clermont Ferrand, 1st Oct. 1732, died 17th September 1785. He was one of a family of seventeen children. A perusal of *Jumonville* is calculated to induce the reader to believe that there were not brains enough to go round, for though not very long,—the four cantos contain less than a thousand lines in all,—it is hopelessly dull and uninteresting, never rising to pathos, though often sinking to bathos. The couplet describing the death of *Jumonville* will serve as an example:
  Par un plomb homicide indignement percé,
  Aux pieds de ses boureaux il tombe renversé.

There is no mention of Washington in the poem;—either the poet had never heard of him at the time (1759) or could not make the name fit into his verses.

Note D, page 63.

The author is not quite fair towards Frederick Howard, 5th Earl of Carlisle (b. 1748, d. 1825). Though a fop in his early days,—he and Fox were esteemed the two best dressed men in town,—he developed into a fairly good statesman, with a cultivated literary taste. He is, perhaps, best known as the guardian of Lord Byron, who dedicated the "Hours of Idleness" to him, abused him in "English Bards and Scotch Reviewers," ("The paralytic puling of Carlisle") and made the *amende honorable*, in "Childe Harold" c. iii, 29, 30. His reply to La Fayette's challenge was not quite as given by our author, but was to the effect that "he considered himself solely responsible to his country and king, and not to an individual." It is quite true that the opposition papers in England made sarcastic remarks about him, and no doubt, if he still continued to wear paint and patches, the fact was not forgotten. Horace Walpole said of him, that, "he was very fit to make a treaty that will not be made."

Note E, page 64.

If Charles Hector, Comte d'Estaing (b. 1729) had been able to do the English half the harm that he wished them, they would have been swept off the face of the earth. The cause of his animosity was not very creditable to him. He was taken prisoner by the English at the siege of Madras (he was then a soldier) and released on parole. He broke his parole, and at the head of a party of Frenchmen "did a good deal of harm to English commerce." He was again captured, and as his word was obviously of no value, he was sent to England, and spent some time in Portsmouth Jail. When he was released he returned to France, "vowing eternal hatred to the English," though as his French biographer owns, "his not very loyal conduct had provoked the punishment under which he groaned." He was appointed Admiral in 1763. He did not achieve any very remarkable feat in American waters, against Howe. In the Revolution he tried to "sit on the fence," but there was a short method with mugwumps in those days, and he was brought before the tribunal and condemned to death, 28th April 1794.

Note F, page 65.

Pierre André de Suffren Saint-Tropez, generally called Bailli de Suffren, was one of the best and bravest sailors France ever had. He was born at St. Cannat, in Provence,

13th July 1726, died 8th December 1788. He opposed the English in the East, and in 1782 fought five obstinately contested naval battles with Admiral Sir Edward Hughes. Of these battles Professor Laughton says (*Dict. Nat. Biog.*), "There is no other instance in naval history of two fleets thus fighting five battles within little more than a year (four of them within seven months) with no very clear advantage on either side. French writers speak of the five battles as 'five glorious victories,' but in reality they were very evenly balanced in point of fighting, whilst as to strategic results, the English had a slight advantage from the first three, the French from the last two. The tactical advantage, however, commonly lay with the French, who were prevented from reaping the benefit of it solely by the mutinous or cowardly conduct of the French captains." It is possible that De Suffren would not have fared so well if pitted against Rodney, Hood, or Howe, but at any rate he would have shown himself a fearless fighter and a skilful seaman—a veritable "sea-dog" of a type which, unfortunately for France, has been all too rare in the annals of her navy.

Note G, page 70.

The letter given is quite characteristic of its writer, and though not included in Lomenie's valuable Life of Beaumarchais, is no doubt genuine, being exactly in the sarcastic strain he would be likely to employ. Of his quarrel with Congress this is not the place to speak, but we cannot unreservedly accept the Chevalier de Pontgibaud's estimation of him.

Note II, page 87.

François Joseph Paul, Comte de Grasse (b. 1723) though a brave man was not a great tactician. He was also unfortunate in being opposed to Hood, whom Nelson called, "the best officer, take him altogether, that England had to boast of." In Jan. 1782 De Grasse, with 32 ships, allowed Hood, with only 23, to get into the harbour at St. Christophers, take 1300 men who were being besieged there, and get out again unscathed. Three months later, Rodney and Hood inflicted a heavy defeat on De Grasse, sinking his flag ship and taking him prisoner. Anglo-Saxons always respect a brave man, and De Grasse was treated more like a guest than a prisoner whilst in England. On his release he returned to France, but did not again assume the command of a squadron, and died in Paris, 14th Jan. 1788, in the 65th year of his age.

Note I, page 88.

Armand Louis de Gontaut Biron, Duc de Lauzun, born 15th April 1747, died on the scaffold 31st Dec. 1793. His youth was passed in dissipation, but in 1777, he startled everybody by bringing out a pamphlet on "The State of Defence of England and her Possessions in all the four quarters of the World," which led to his being entrusted with the command of an expedition to destroy the English settlements on the coast of Senegal. This he successfully accomplished (Jan. 1779), and in 1780 he was fighting in America. He took the Revolutionary side, and received the command of the Army of the Rhine in 1792, and in 1793 was employed against the Vendeans. As a matter of course he was accused of uncitizenly conduct "and too much moderation towards the rebels," was deprived of his command, imprisoned, condemned, and executed.

Note J, page 101.

Philippe Pinel a celebrated doctor, distinguished for his knowledge of mathematics and philosophy, but best known for having introduced the humane treatment of the insane, who until that time had been treated as dangerous animals, and left to rot neglected in noisome dungeons. He was the author of over twenty scientific works. He died 25th Oct. 1826.

Note K, page 104.

When Louis XIV, was shown the newly-completed palace of Trianon, he asked De Louvois, who was not only Prime Minister, but "Inspector of Royal Buildings" why one of the windows was smaller than the others? De Louvois rudely declared that they were all the same size. The King said nothing, but the next day sent for Le Nôtre, a celebrated artist and architect, and asked him in the presence of De Louvois whether the windows were all the same size? Le Nôtre declared that one of them was a trifle smaller than the others, and the King turned in triumph towards De Louvois. The Minister went home in a rage. "I must give this young fool something better to think about than the size of windows," he said, and within the next few hours he had declared war against Holland. The story is of doubtful authenticity, but if not true is *ben trovato*.

Note L, page 107.

Marie Jean Hérault de Seychelles, who owing to influence at Court, obtained several good appointments. In the Revolution he became a Girondin, was a follower of Danton, and perished with his leader and Camille Desmoulins on the scaffold.

Note M, page 128.

In spite of the author's prejudices Moreau de St. Mery must be deemed a good man;—in fact if it may be said that La Fayette was the only man who "kept his head" in the Revolution, it might also be averred that Moreau de St. Mery was the only man who kept his heart. He was born in the island of Martinique, 13th Jan. 1750. When he was only three years old he lost his father, and his mother would not let him go to France to be educated. His grandfather was a judge or magistrate, and young Moreau de St. Mery was when a boy, always interceding for some unfortunate prisoner. At his grandfather's death he inherited a sum of money, destined to defray the cost of his legal education in France, but he used the money to pay the old man's debts. At the age of nineteen he came to Paris, and studied hard. He resolved to sleep only one night in three. He acquired in fourteen months such a knowledge of Latin that he wrote a thesis in that language, and could declaim long passages, not only from the works of the poets, but from treatises on law, etc. During the first part of the Revolution he entered the National Assembly as representative of Martinique, but he was far too moderate or good-hearted. He was attacked whilst returning home one night, and left for

dead on the pavement, with half a dozen sabre cuts on
his head and body. He recovered, and retired to the
little village of Forges, where he was arrested by the spies
of the Terror. One of these bravos, however, helped him
to escape, and he got to Havre, where hearing that
Robespierre had issued fresh orders for his arrest, he
sailed for America. He kept a book-store and printing
business at Philadelphia. The author's statement that he
had little or no stock in his shop, and failed for a large
amount, is not confirmed by the biographical dictionaries,
which assert that he lived in some style at Philadelphia,
and was often able to help poor French emigrants. He
returned to France and was employed by Napoleon on
several missions, but he was too soft-hearted, and having
remonstrated with Junot for having burned a few villages
and slaughtered the inhabitants, he was recalled from
Parma, the seat of his last mission. Napoleon did not
employ him again, and did not pay him his salary.
Moreau de St. Mery sought an interview with the Emperor.
"I do not expect you to recompense my honesty," he
said, "only to recognize it. Do not be afraid," he added
sarcastically, "the disease is not contagious." Napoleon
nevertheless allowed him to nearly starve, but, at the
Restoration, Louis XVIII gave him 15,000 francs, and this
enabled him to pay his few debts and pass the remainder
of his days in comfort. He died 28th Jan. 1819, aged 69.
The motto of his life, and to which he always acted up,
was "*Il est toujours l'heure de faire le bien.*"

Note N, page 132.

Louis Marie, Vicomte de Noailles (born 1756) fought in
the War of Independence. Like many others of the

"gilded youth" of France, he imbibed in America revolutionary notions which he carried back to France, and in the Revolution he was one of the most "advanced" members of the Convention. At last he found he could not conscientiously follow the leaders of the people, and in May, 1792 he went to England, expecting a change in affairs to soon take place. Then came the " 10th August," and De Noailles was shortly afterwards proscribed as an *émigré*. His father, mother, and wife were guillotined. To return was impossible, so he went to the United States and settled at Philadelphia, where he became a partner in the banking house of Bingham and Co. He learned to speak English so well that on one occasion he conducted a law-suit that lasted fifteen days. Towards the close of the year 1800 his name was removed from the list of *émigrés*, but his business affairs in the United States were so extensive that he refused to return to France. In 1803 he went to Hayti on business, and there met Rochambeau who entrusted him with the command of a fort garrisoned by 1800 men, but which was blockaded by a British squadron, whilst " 20,000 blacks" (?) besieged it by land. Rochambeau, who commanded the main army of some 5000 men, was forced to capitulate, but was allowed to transport his troops to Cuba. De Noailles was summoned to surrender, but he replied that " a French general who had provisions, ammunition, and devoted soldiers could not surrender without shame." He had been privately informed that Rochambeau's convoy would pass near his fort on a certain night, and he cleverly got all his men on board ship, ran out under cover of the darkness and joined Rochambeau without being perceived by any of the British vessels. They got to Cuba, but De Noailles wished to join a French force at Havannah. He

and a company of grenadiers who were faithful to him,
embarked on board a small French ship, called the *Courrier*,
mounting only four small guns. They fell in with a
British sloop of war, the *Hazard*, 7 guns. De Noailles
displayed the British flag, and when hailed replied in such
excellent English that the captain of the *Hazard* was
deceived, and asked if they had seen anything of "General
de Noailles" whom the *Hazard* had been commissioned
to capture. De Noailles replied that he was on the same
errand, and he would accompany the *Hazard*. In the
middle of the night he ran his vessel into the *Hazard*
and boarded her. The English though taken by surprise,
fought well, and though the *Hazard* was captured De
Noailles was mortally wounded, and many of his men
killed. De Noailles died of his wounds a week later (9th
Jan. 1804) at Havannah. His heart was enclosed in a
silver box, and his grenadiers attached it to their flag and
carried it back to France.

Note O, page 133.

There is not much difficulty in identifying the "Bishop
of A——" with Charles Maurice de Talleyrand, Bishop
of Autun. The particulars of his life are so well known
that there is no need to recapitulate them here, but a few
words may be said about his attempt to "blackmail" the
United States Envoys. It is perfectly true that Talleyrand
extorted bribes from everybody who was willing to pay
him, and that he called the sums he so received *douceurs*.
The "negociators" from the United States—Messrs. Charles
Cotesworth Pinckney, John Marshall, and Elbridge Gerry,
—had not been long in Paris before they were informed
by a Mr. Bellamy (said to be a partner with Talleyrand

in this blackmailing business) Ste Foix, and a lady, who cannot easily be identified, that "nothing could be done without money; the members of the Directory must be paid." According to the popular story, Pinckney replied. "War be it then. Millions for defence but not a cent for tribute." This does not quite agree with the Chevalier's statement that he heard one of he Envoys,—probably Pinckney,—inform Congress that they had paid Talleyrand 50,000 francs, and only stopped when they found the blackmailers but increased their demands the more they received. I cannot help fancying that the popular version is the correct one; it accords more with the dignity of the American people, and is borne out by the undoubted fact that Talleyrand was frightened, and wrote to Mr. Pinckney to ask the names of the persons who had demanded money, who, he alleged, had done so without any authority from him. Talleyrand did not display his usual cunning in the transaction, for his letter aroused the wrath of Bellamy, who thereupon wrote to Mr. Gerry, that, "he had done nothing, said nothing, and written nothing without the instructions of Citizen Talleyrand."

The "woman of colour" to whom the Chevalier alludes, was doubtless Madame Grand, "an Indian beauty" who was Talleyrand's mistress for many years, and whom he would have married if he had not been prevented by the unalterable formula of the Roman Catholic Church, "once a priest, always a priest." She survived him by a few years, and is buried in the Montparnasse Cemetery, at Paris.

Note P, page 142.

Constantin François Chasseboeuf, Comte de Volney was a well known philosopher and author. His "Ruins" was once a popular book. It involved him in a discussion with Dr. Priestley who called him," an atheist, an ignoramus, a Chinese, and a Hottentot." His theories have long since fallen into desuetude in France and oblivion elsewhere, and it is therefore unnecessary to criticize them here. His name still remains familiar to most travelled Americans, as a street in Paris is called after him.

Note Q, page 142.

The Princes d'Orléans mentioned in these pages were Louis Philippe and his two brothers. Louis Philippe arrived in America towards the end of 1796, and was joined by his brothers early in 1797. After spending some time in America they left for England, where they lived on an allowance from the British Government until the Restoration.

Note R, page 187.

The Chevalier, writing many years after the events occurred, has rather mixed up his dates. Of the Duke of Ragusa (Marmont) who was the first governor of Illyria he says nothing. General J. is, of course, Junot. He went out of his mind, and it is most likely he was kidnapped in the manner stated. A very few months later he threw himself out of window, fractured his thigh and died of the effects of the consequent amputation,— July, 1813. "General B——,"—who preceded, not followed Junot, as the Chevalier states,—was Bertrand. There were several officers of this name. The one mentioned, I believe, was not the Bertrand who accompanied Napoleon to St. Helena, but a skilful engineer, who was removed from his command in Illyria and sent to fortify Antwerp, and render it—"a pistol held at the breast of England." He afterwards resided in the United States where he undertook several important engineering works. Joseph Fouché, Duke of Otranto was such a well-known personage that he will be found mentioned in any good biographical dictionary.

Note S, page 190.

Gustavus IV was only 14 when he succeeded his father. An intense hatred of the French, or rather Napoleon made him almost a monomaniac, and involved his country in wars with both France and Russia, with defeat and loss of territory in both cases. He was at last deposed and the throne given to his uncle the Duke of Sudermania. Gustavus wandered about Europe under the names of Comte Gottorp, or Duke of Holstein-Eutin, and after 1816, called himself simply "Gustafson", or the son of Gustavus. It is possible that he was a congenital lunatic, and his misfortunes aggravated the disease. An instance of his eccentricity is the curious advertisement which he inserted in all the leading journals of Europe previous to starting for the Holy Land. He advertised for ten travelling companions, viz., an Englishman, a Dane, a Spaniard, a Frenchman, a Hungarian, a Dutchman, an Italian, a Russian, a Swiss, and an inhabitant of Holstein-Eutin. They were all to have good certificates as to morals and character, and each was to bring 4000 florins, or at least 2000 florins, to be put to a common fund. They were all to dress in black robes, to let their beards grow "as a sign of their manly resolution;" and they were to be known as the Black Brotherhood. They were to meet at Trieste on a certain day. Apparently the people of Europe were disinclined to avail themselves of the privilege of a trip to Palestine in the company of a royal "crank," for no one answered this extraordinary advertisement, and Gustavus started off by himself,—but soon returned. He retired to Switzerland, where he lived in the greatest poverty, for he refused to receive any money from Sweden, and would have starved had not his divorced queen and children contrived without his knowledge to supply his wants. He died in 1837 in such obscurity that there are even doubts as to the place of his death. An English encyclopædia says that he died at St. Gall in Switzerland;—a French one that he died in Moravia.

Note T, page 191.

Jérôme Bonaparte, the youngest brother of Napoleon I, was born at Ajaccio, Nov., 1784, and died at Villegenis (Seine et Oise) 24th June, 1860. He came to France at an early age, and, after a very little schooling had been wasted upon him, was given a commission in the Consular Guards. A quarrel and a duel, with the son of General Davout, caused him to quit the army and join the navy. In 1803 he visited the United States, where he married Miss Patterson, but the marriage was declared null and void by the Emperor.

After seeing some naval service, he returned to France and was eventually received into the favour of his elder brother, given the command of an army corps, and eventually created king of Westphalia and married the Princess Catharine of Wurtemberg. He was a mere "Carnival King," and indulged in every sort of dissipation, took baths of Bordeaux wine, bestowed enormous gifts of money on his male and female favourites, and wasted nearly a quarter of the revenues of his extensive kingdom in vice and debauchery.

When the fall of the Empire seemed imminent, he at first thought of joining his brother's enemies, but finding that such a step would bring him nothing but disgrace, retired first to France, and then to Trieste, with his wife, who still refused to leave him.

After Napoleon's escape from Elba, Jérôme again rejoined his brother, and fought gallantly at Charleroi, Quatre-Bras and Waterloo. Imprisoned along with his wife by the Allies, he was after a few months set free, and went to reside first at Naples, then at Trieste, Rome, and Florence. In 1847 he was permitted to return to France. He took no part in the Revolution of 1848 beyond giving it his "moral support," but favoured the ambitious views of his nephew, who, in return created him Governor of the Invalides, a Marshal of France, and after the *Coup d'État*, President of the Senate. He took little or no part in politics, however, and was almost forgotten by the public when he died in 1860.

FURTHER CRITICAL NOTES

At the moment of going to press with this second edition, we were favoured with the following kind letter from a courteous correspondent across the Atlantic. It was then too late to make any changes in the body of the book, we, therefore, reproduce our friend's corrections here, and trust they will make the Chevalier's Memoirs historically more complete.

BROOKLYN, New York.
September 30, 1897.

ROBERT B. DOUGLAS Esq,
PARIS.

DEAR SIR:—

I have read with much interest your translation of "A French Volunteer of the War of Independence". There is a great deal in it to arrest the attention of the reader, and while it would not change history, the book would certainly serve to illustrate it.

When we consider the time that intervened between the happening of the events he recorded, and the writing of the memoirs, we must admire his memory. Permit me to point out a few lapses, the result doubtless of a want of full acquaintance, on the part of the author, with American geography and biography. When a second edition appears the corrections might appear as foot notes, and pending that, you could mark them with a pen in your private copy. They are surprisingly few.

Pages 37, 38, 39, 40, 47, 51, Valley Forges should be Valley Forge.

Page 39. Mr. Jefferson's signature was T. Jefferson, never Jefferson: but the T and the J were somewhat intertwined, and the Chevalier might easily have mistaken the reading.

Page 44. The date left blank should be 1755.

Page 55. Rareton should be Raritan. In all probability an error of typography in the original French. Lower case o and e are often confounded in manuscript, and the omission of a dot might make an i seem like an *e*. There is little doubt the Chevalier wrote Raritan correctly, and the printers made a blunder. Such names were strange to French eyes, ears and pens.

Page 71. The Continental Congress was a much larger body than the author supposes. What he refers to is the Committee of Congress which sat during the recess of the Congress, for routine business, and consisted of one member from each State. To this Committee were confided certain duties which it is unnecessary to recapitulate here.

Page 100. The Society of the Cincinnati. It still exists, the present members being the descendants of original members, who were officers of the Continental Army; the right to wear its Eagle and ribbon is jealously guarded, and membership therein is held in high esteem.

Page 145. Akensie should be Hackensack, and Topanah should be Tappan. Here memory was treacherous with the Chevalier, and there was no Gazetteer to refer to.

Page 146. Burgh should be Burr. Aaron Burr is meant.

I trust you will take in good part these suggestions of mine. Mr. Carrington is to be congratulated on having produced such an admirable specimen of typography, and you ought to be thanked by every American for giving them the opportunity to read the book in the language they know best.

Very truly yours,

JOHN. E. NORCROSS.

www.ingramcontent.com/pod-product-compliance
Lightning Source LLC
Chambersburg PA
CBHW031819230426
43669CB00009B/1189